Where Is Paradise Found?

Paradise Found

- Recognizing and Living As The Infinite Love That You Are -

By Charlie Hayes

"Paradise Found"

First Edition

ISBN 978-09766619-4-8

Contact: Charlie Hayes

Enid OK USA - +1 580 366-4083

www.theeternalstate.org

non.duality@yahoo.com

Other books by Charlie Hayes:

Nonduality:

"From I Am to I Am, With Love"

"Perfect Peace"

"Life After Death"

"No Way Out"

Business:

"Get Sponsored "

(A guide For Racers Seeking Corporate Sponsorships)

Dedicated to all "Seekers of Truth" everywhere everywhen

May your seeking end right now … and Nothing be found…

Paradise is Here. You cannot get Here from Here.

Only Love Is Real.
All Else Is Imagination.

- Charlie Hayes -
Enid, Oklahoma, USA

21 July, 2008

Table Of Contents

Gratitude

First off to, thanks to my family for enduring my proselytizing while I was still searching as I found such amazing pointers and ill-advisedly tried to convince myself by convincing them!

Secondly, thanks to Maury Lee for some excellent editing.

Finally, I have great timeless gratitude for those who generously and unswervingly pointed out the unperceivable obvious inconceivable truth, beyond description, beyond language, beyond the beyond (whatever THAT is!) …

Swami Muktananda Paramahamsa

Sri Ramana Maharshi

Werner Erhard

Sri Sri Ravi Shankar

Wayne ("Ram Tzu") Liquorman

Ramesh Balsekar

Leo Hartong

Byron Katie

Jeff Foster

Tony Parsons

Unmani (Liza) Hyde

Stephen Wingate

Annette Nibley …

Sri Nisargadatta Maharaj

AND The "Final Teacher", John Wheeler.

Especially, I must express an undying unborn immensity of Gratitude, Respect and Love for my Timeless Friends" …

John Wheeler … John's website is at www.thenaturalstata.org (By far the best expression, always fresh and up to date pointers from The One Self – Who You Really Are).

John is also the author of "Awakening To The Natural State", "Shining In Plain View", "Right Here Right Now", and "You Were Never Born". All are available on Amazon.com. And all highly recommended.

'Sailor' Bob Adamson … And a most Amazing expression, who provided some much needed "ruthless compassion" and "uncompromising love" with a precision and timing that can only come from The One Who Abides As That…

And Finally,

John Greven … Who, along with John Wheeler and 'Sailor' Bob, provided a few final pushes to a stubborn ego belief, out of mind into nowhere. (John Greven is the author of "Oneness" – 'The Destination You Never Left' and his website is www.onenessjustthat.com. Highly recommended.)

One such potent pointer can be found in the introduction to this book. Get that one and the search for meaning and knowledge ends in the Full Stop of Eternity.

All are Best Friends In Forever… Paradise Found.

Q: What is the point of this book

A. There is no point. That is the point.

Foreword - By Stephen Wingate

With the power and force of a sledge-hammer, Charlie's words strike to the core of the mind destroying all false images and beliefs. His intensity is palpable. Having all misconceptions crushed, the reader has no way out and is left in their natural state of peace and well-being.

Charlie is tenacious and relentless in his communication of the message of nonduality. And his relentless tenacity comes as no surprise—he's lived his entire life in the fast-lane. Whether he's racing cars, selling Ferraris, playing Jazz or sharing the message of Oneness, he does it with energy, passion and love.

If you find yourself seeking and suffering, introduce yourself to the Nondual sledge-hammer called Charlie Hayes, and you just may find your spiritual search is over.

(Stephen's website is www.livinginpeace-thenaturalstate.com)

A Comment - by Unmani (Liza) Hyde

Charlie's book 'Paradise Found' is such a clear and direct expression which points to who you really are beyond all concepts. This can never be known or understood. Charlie is so good at pointing out that the mind can never 'get this', even though it continues to try, again and again! This is a book that you can dip in and out of as you feel, each time being redirected back to who you really are - Life itself.

(Unmani's website is www.not-knowing.com; the book is 'I Am Life Itself'.)

A Review - By Scott Kiloby

Something strikes you the moment you start reading Paradise Found by Charlie Hayes, which is the full force of the relentless message here. Charlie is pointing in a no holds barred way to a truth so real, it is literally everywhere as One Truth, as you and me and everything we see, and yet it is nothing at all. This truth is therefore inexpressible. Yet, Charlie is expressing something that every so-called teacher ought to have the guts to say, which is: Do you see the bullshit? Do you realize that your belief in this or that is no different than a belief in Santa Claus? These are pointers that allow the reader to look for himself or herself and discover there is no self.

In the foreword, Stephen Wingate poignantly refers to Charlie's writing as having "the power and force of a sledge hammer." What is so amazingly beautiful, however, is that after you take that sledge hammer within, and allow it to destroy every belief, what is left is genuine, "unconditioned, unbounded love." Charlie points to and hammers on what is essentially an illusory story of lack called "me," which then reveals the abundance inherent in nothingness. Only a genuine transformation beyond concepts could embrace the seemingly paradoxical nature of such a realization.

With his signature ruthless compassion, Charlie states, "Keep seeking Paradise. That will make it absolutely certain that you will NEVER find Paradise." This kind of powerful and direct pointer leaves no room to hide within a concept about this one inexpressible truth called "enlightenment" or non-duality. It allows the reader to see the futility of the search, to see that the search is the self, and that the self is much ado about nothing. In seeing that futility, the possibility of true spiritual awakening arises, the kind that realizes that even the concept of awakening is bullcrap. This is the total deconstruction and demolition of what you believe to be truth. Only the real, totally liberating and loving truth could be that generous.

(Scott Kiloby is the author of "Love's Quiet Revolution: The End Of The Spiritual Search". His website is www.kiloby.com.)

A Review - By Maury Lee

''Paradise Found' is a book you can read over and over. I guarantee you, Charlie stays on point. This book doesn't waver, it doesn't examine 5,000 ideas. Just One. As many seekers have said, "I needed to keep getting hit with the same brick". Charlie Hayes uses just One brick, over and over, in different ways. It's dependable. It works.

Charlie Hayes is one who will not ask you to believe anything. All his writing is only pointing out "bullshit." Only right looking leads you away from the "bullshit." In this book, Charlie reminds you not to take his writing as Truth. He knows that all words fail. His words point you to seeing No Thing. In this he succeeds.

There is no current teacher (my descriptive term) that speaks more plainly, more directly, than Charlie Hayes. Tough love is an understatement. Charlie has the unsophisticated mind of Nisargadatta. If he calls you an 'idiot,' pay attention.

Charlie's forte is knowing that we don't know what we don't know. Seeing this is his major effort. HOW TO LOOK. This book will help you see what you've missed in all your reading, in all your ideas. His writing makes it clear that "you don't know that you don't know.

Paradise Found is full of Charlie's sense of humor. The humor lets you know that this is spoken with ease. It's only hard and serious until no one gets it. Please, let Charlie laugh at you. Perhaps you'll start laughing too. The sophisticated seeker wants answers. Charlie only asks, "Who's asking?" When you can't find who's asking, Charlie's book has done its work.

One thing about this book, it doesn't waver, it doesn't stray; it stays right on point. Tough Love and bullshit don't sit well together. Charlie's "Emperor" has no clothes. He will make it clear that you are naked awareness only. If you want to keep your clothes, don't read this book. If you do read it, and get hit by this bus, you will surely be in Paradise.

(Maury's website is http://nomaury.blogspot.com)

Only Love is Eternal.

All else is a Passing Show ...

Arising and subsiding

Here in this timeless moment...

IN That Eternal Love that You are!

~

This Is Paradise Found

Just This

As It Is.

Introduction

I. Disclaimer

As this book was being written the "author" came to see that what this book points to simply cannot be described, expressed, written, shared, represented, languaged, understood, experienced, or known - by the "author", or "anyone else".

Therefore the "seeing here" is that the writing - and the reading – of these words, shall be ultimately known as absolutely FUTILE.

(But who would know that it's futile? Ha!)

So how is it that this book came out - in spite of that seeing?

Perhaps we should ask the legendary sage and author of an appearing ponderation in language called "The Tao", one "Lao Tzu" .....

According to legend (or translation and are these not the same?) Lao Tzu may have said (depending on which of the billion translations you come onto), "The Tao that can be spoken of is not the enduring and unchanging Tao."

Then if that is a pointer to Reality, why did this Lao Tzu guy go on to write eighty or more verses of elegant yet pointless points?

Guess we'll have to ask him. But wait he's dead.

Now what?

Guess we'll have to ask US. If we can find such a one.

II. Redundant Warning

Nothing in this book is real.

Nothing in this book is true.

This book points to something you do not know that you do not know. That is not a thing that words can describe, evoke, or represent.

Without one or more of those, what is left?

Nothing.

Also "known" by "no-one" as

Paradise.

The Timeless Abode You Never Left.

Q: How do I tell the truth from the false?

C. That's easy. It's ALL false.

As my dear friend John Greven, author of "Oneness," notes: "Here's a 'Litmus Test' - If ANYTHING is assumed to be other than bullshit – then there is something wrong with the perspective".

So? So: There IS no "true perspective".

Full Stop.

Part One: A Priori Awareness

Prior to

I Am

You Are

No

Thing

What Is The Real You?

Some call This that you ARE

"Ordinary Awareness".

Nothing special at all.

The fullness of Emptiness

This Emptiness of the Fullness

Just That and Everything Else

Just This and Nothing Else

Words! Get Thee Behind Me!

Words! Begone!

Words Be FUN

1. Being and Reality

You Are Unborn - Empty Loving Awareness

See if you can actually find a separate entity you call "me" in direct, actual experience. Look and see. Are you REALLY separate or is that just a story you have believed like you used to believe in Santa Claus? Paradise is found when YOU are lost! And the funny thing is, you were never born. Only an idea arrived and you mistook that idea of "me" apart from "other" to be what you are. But that's a LIE! Cannot accept this? Then ask WHO cannot accept this. But you can't force Grace, That (The Real YOU) is more Real than the false idea of a separate I, so allow That to erase the false, as That will, as best you can. Relax and ask. Drop all answers, only ask. Am I? WHO Am I? Am I? What Am I? Am I?

"How can you speak or develop any concept unless the primary concept 'I am' is available? This primary concept begets further concepts; that is all other concepts occur to it. However, whatever concept occurs to you, including the primary concept 'I am', is not the eternal state".

"I know exactly how transient this present state of affairs is, and I also know the eternal state. I have no use for this ephemeral state. I understand the false as false. Since I have found my true permanent state I have no need for any of this; it has come on its own and it will go on its own. In that fullness there is no need of any kind. I've had that state of fullness after I met my guru; if I hadn't met him I would have lived and died as an ordinary man". - *Sri Nisargadatta Maharaj (courtesy of Pradeep Apte, aptep@yahoo.com.)*

Me too :-)

2. Was Wholeness Ever Lost?

Who claims "I am not whole and complete"?

Who claims I did something right and got the outcome I wanted so now I am happy?

Who claims I did something wrong and got the outcome I didn't want so now I am unhappy?

Who thinks This Is Not paradise?

Who thinks?

WHO?

Paradise cannot be found by you.

Paradise was never lost! How can what is not lost be found?

Can a thing that has no actual existence (you) ever discover that which is not lost?

Ponder this.

3. What Is Unreal? What Is Real?

The Basics of it...

1. YOU are Awareness, simply being. No one can say they do not exist. That existence, the sense of "I" as in "I Am," is undeniable and inescapable. Try to NOT BE. Cannot be done. So the simple pointer is, what you are IS That Presence of Awareness. YOU ARE. Being. Just That! This True You ... BE-ING... is POINTED TO in language with concepts like Impersonal Consciousness; Awareness, The Absolute, The Ultimate Timeless Subject, or Not one Not two ... YOU are just THAT, prior to the mind's translation into the thought I Am and I am this or that.

2. You are NOT an "individual." There are NO "individuals" anywhere except in unreal dream-like stories. The idea of a separate person is a fiction, a mind-construction, a house of cards, as the story tries to say, I'm ME! (Unsuccessfully!) This idea of a "me" is ... on investigation ... seen to be a false claim by the thinking machinery to its own separate existence. This ever-changing idea of a person is simply unreal. WHO says "I'm Me?" The mind. To be blunt, it's bullshit. The whole fabricated story of me is pure bullshit: all stories of "individuals" are actually a fiction. As Shakespeare said, it's a tale told by an idiot, filled with sound and fury, signifying ... NOTHING.

3. Let all thoughts drop into the Nothing from where they bubbled up, except Who Am I?

The Core False Assumption

Q: I remember you had mentioned that "I" comes into play at the age of 2. I want your opinion on what would be a good way to raise a kid. A cousin of mine has a 2 year old kid. What advice would you give to raise a kid so that the kid lives a life of free of suffering?"

C. The assumption here is that there is some ability to control what happens.

There is not.

There is NO person.

When that is recognized fully all ideas of advising and opining become what they are ... nonsense.

I suggest that you look at who asked this question? Who would give advice and to whom?

All questions based on that core false premise, the erroneous assumption of "personhood," will only always yield false "answers"! :-)

Can An Idea Do Or Know ANYThing?

Q: I have a question about the Unknowable. Sometimes you refer to it as happening to No one, nothing, emptiness etc. I know they are just words. But then you say it is Oneness, which implies there is Someone, and only that Someone who is in charge who is appearing to make things appear. Are these terms not confusing to us who are still suffering from the afflictions of the idea of a separate person?

C. Who asks these questions?

WHO claims "I am confused" or "we" are confused? What mechanism claims "We are suffering"? Where IS this "us"? Unless you think there is an us, there IS no us. That is only a thought, an idea. You take an idea – a thought! - to be solid and real and THAT is the fundamental error of the seeker mind. But LOOK: Can an IDEA actually know or do anything at all? No. See that one right now!

You assume you are a thought, the idea "I am," and then try to get some "right concept" to add to the false, which merely reinforces the false (!) ... and that is never going to work because there ARE no "right concepts". ALL are words that point to that which is beyond comprehension. What YOU are is PRIOR to al concepts and all experiences; YOU ARE and prior to language.

And that is not "true" either! IT IS A POINTER and NOT some new thing to believe.

What is missing is investigation: Look in that space of awareness there and see right now …Where is that assumed solid personal entity? Without assuming you are an idea in

24

mind, where ARE you? LOOK for that "person" and you find … nothing. You are that nothing, arising as everything.

The mind CANNOT grasp it.

Go beyond thought to what IS - Presence, Awareness, Here Now always and forever timeless spaceless Isness.

THAT is ungraspable.

Try to grasp This with mind and you must fail. It is like trying to tie Space in a knot.

Q: Or have I not heard you properly?

C. When it's "you" trying to "hear another" the message is completely lost in concepts and confusions. So NO; there is NOT yet the hearing of I AM hearing I AM.

See that and ask that one you take to be you, WHO is attempting to grasp the ungraspable!

That is all.

Keep it really really simple! Come back to "The basics" (above) until there is no sense of being a separate entity left to ask and desire knowing for itself.

The 'me' of memory is a mere figment. Except for the word or idea, nothing tangible is present. This recognition kicks the legs out from under the belief for good. It is no use saying 'I know there is no me present' and then returning to stories, doubts or problems about the 'me'! So just see the basic point right now. In truth you are fully, finally, and completely free in this moment and ever. Any other experience is a mere imagined concept that is taking place in the ever-present freedom that you are. The end!

– John Wheeler

4. Illumination

Elimination (of the false) is Illumination (of the Real)

Paraphrasing the Tao, I say, To know your True Nature, the Eternal Unchanging 'Always So', is to be illumined. How is this known? By looking. The urge to Inquiry, Self-Investigation, is a kind of "grace." Good fortune! Awareness of being (I am) happens in Timeless Spaceless Being. This is seen by looking. Look for the one who looks. That is a way of looking. Now. Always NOW.

Look. Where is the knower? Can't find one. Not ever. Seeing this, what can disappear (with "grace") is the belief in the knower. Concepts still arise but without the energy of belief they appear and disappear like clouds. Then (now) - Presence-Awareness, the cognizing emptiness, remains pristine, untouched, unaffected. That is already always the actuality right now; the actual is just overlooked ... until it isn't.

This happens NOW. Where does NOW start? When does HERE begin? This Is It, Here and Now the Self is whole and complete. All is already resolved in this Unborn Cognizing Vacant Self. You ARE That. There is absolutely NO Way Out of Being. This is the Gift of Unknowing ... Total Freedom.

Keep coming back to the simplicity of that which is aware. Right now you are aware of these words. This awareness that's looking out through your eyes is Love. Thoughts, feelings, stories, and dramas all appear to you. You are the Love you're seeking. We are all seeking Love. The great and liberating realization is that we are the Love we are seeking, and it is always here. Just notice—I am the Love I'm seeking. I am Love. I Am.

- Stephen Wingate

The Self is not an experience; it is the experiencing. Like sight can see but never be seen, the experiencing can experience, but not be experienced. You are that experiencing.

- Leo Hartong

5. Only YOU

Out HERE

Out Here in This Field

I Am You

You Are I

Out Here In The Now

Beyond All Dreams Of Being

Here, We Are

In Love

With

Love

No-one knows This.

But when that Bus-Called-Oneness HITS you, all is known naturally and by no knower.

Care to step in front of this bus?

Read ON.

Or not!

Maybe it is best not TO RISK LOSING EVERYTHING you hold dear.

Then again …

WHAT IF That Bus is a one-way trip to Paradise … the Abode You Never Left ………….

Step right this way………

Step into my parlor, said the Spider to the fly!

Fly into Me, dear moth. I welcome you home, come, come, fly into Me, I Am the Love you seek, O dear moth!

What will it cost me to regain Paradise?

Everything!

What is the payoff for NOT coming Home to Paradise?

Consider this:

To sell Love out to be right, to win, to dominate, to avoid domination, to justify "self" and invalidate "other", is simply the disease of the Mind Of Humanity.

Examples of this are stunningly abundant. Read the news. Watch a political discussion between two pundits from the extremes of left or right wing viewpoints.

All perspectives are false. No perspective is real. ONLY No-Perspective is Real. :-) Oneness is what you ARE and That is NOT a concept NOR an experience. NOT a "perspective". All of that comes and goes on the screen of Awareness Itself ... The One That IS... This Timeless Love that is simply beyond description.

This mechanistic human doingness (doing not being) that we call "mind" lives in the imaginary infamy of a zealous need to argue and win over what it perceives to be those poor ignorant ones to ITS point of view, ITS perspective.

This can bring an experience of deep sadness laced with a ruthless compassion that might lash out in what looks to a mind like anger or outrage (as Sri Nisargadatta often demonstrated! Many a disrespectful seeker got tossed out of that loft in Bombay; that is well documented.)

To be self-righteous, judgmental and argumentative with the Love that WILL ultimately burn away that mind-stuff is a rather desperate ploy of the ego's last stand

Sri Nisargadatta and those who reaped the benefits of his pointers and his ruthless Love had no time for fools. The true expression will simply NOT suffer fools who value being right over being Freedom Itself ... not gladly nor otherwise! I speak from experience, having got kicked out of a fine teacher's meetings and told to NEVER return ... owing to that kind of ego-ing behavior of the imaginary 'me'!

And I simply adore that guy now. Wayne Liquorman doesn't need to allow me into his presence. So what I am not welcome at his satsang? There is no-one left to care one way or the other. The seeing is, this that is Real IS Real everywhere and everywhen. So it is that only This Love is Real. ALL else is imagination! Including the imaginary characters called Wayne and Charlie.

So, I cannot help but love Wayne as the Self I Am.

This authentic expression is quite simply, Ruthless Love in action. If a "you" objects and fights the expression then that organism identified as a "you" is a being lived in a loss of paradise, by a false sense of self that was never real and will never win. Love WILL destroy anything unlike Itself, and that happens Just Now.

So the message is, as best "you" can let Love win! Die now. BE the Infinite Love that you are and don't give that diamond away for the paltry and dubious gifts of being RIGHT.

To be right is to be dead to what is possible.

Be Love or be Dead Right. If there is a choice who would NOT choose Infinite LOVE?

Good question.

Ponder this. Who chooses to be right rather than be Love-In-Action? Who indeed.

Who are you? Are you a thing apart from Love? If you believe so, then where is that "one apart" from Love? Where is that "one who is right who just knows that another is wrong"?

ALL points of view are false. Not "wrong" … just flat FALSE.

Look within. Find out what is real and right now, right here, abandon once and forever the dream of not-love that desires to be right and loses paradise in the bargain. That is a bad bargain!

You don't need to do anything to be free.

You are already free.

-Stephen Wingate

THIS IS IT.

As IT Is.

As IT Is Not.

Beyond Both Being and Not-Being….

THIS IS Paradise FOUND.

But ………..

Let's be clear.

Paradise CANNOT be found!

Paradise was NEVER LOST.

This is the Paradox that cannot be resolved.

- From I Am to I Am

6. Don't Believe Any Of This

Q: There is way more peace now. Still back and forth. But more "back" than "forth". Last night after reading the quote below...

"Most people's activities are valueless, if not outright destructive. Dominated by desire and fear, they can do nothing good. Ceasing to do evil precedes beginning to do good. Hence the need for stopping all activities for a time, to investigate one's urges and their motives, see all that is false in one's life, purge the mind of all evil and then only restart work, beginning with one's obvious duties".

With no desire or fear, there seems to me nothing that can be done. If the business website is updated or anything for business is done it is from a desire to make the business better. Without fear there seems to be no desire. Without the desire to give a gift, no gift would be bought. Without desire there seems to be no fear. Good and Evil. Without the "I" there seems to be no "good" or "evil". Any word that could be shared would be appreciated for I feel the hamster wheel beginning to turn.

C. Be careful NOT to take the pointers or words of any "sage" or "book" as some truth to be believed! Where is any believer? Where is a person who is attached to or avoiding any desire or fear?

You wrote "It seems to me that there is nothing to be done." Where is this "me?" Does it exist? Do you take a momentary appearing then disappearing movement of energy arising as letters m and e forming into a word "me" to be what you are? That is the only error. The ONLY mistake is to take your Eternal Self to be a temporary thought!

And ... It is NOT that there is "nothing to be done." There is NO-ONE. Then all "doing happens" as always, with no do-er and no effort of thought or emotion... This no-desire no-fear is YOU as What-You-Really-Are and ALL the rest starting from "me" is a dream-like appearance on the Screen of Presence-Awareness and THAT THOU ART.

Given THAT ... what there is in so-called "life" is... ACT as if "you" have free will. Act as if you have control knowing full well that all ideas of a "me" with control or free will are the dream of Being Itself.

Acting as if you have free will is simple... "you" have been doing that your whole life. Knowing your Self as Presence-Awareness and even before That, the Absolute, is NOT a belief and is NOT a "personal matter." As long as there is a seeming person let that person act in its own self-interest... just do what is next as if you can decide or do...

Who Is This "me?"

No-one no-where and that is the Real.

Let 'er rip!

Follow-up: That has helped. Even when reading "Spiritual masters" quotes. They are still only words and words can only point, and are NOT The Absolute. Hence the saying the Tao that can be spoken is not the Tao and why the truest answer to any question about this is ...Who is asking. That is the answer to all of the questions that have arisen during this. "I" see now why you use it so much and why it is so frustrating to the mind. This time it was not frustrating at all. Just relief. Thank you!

C. You are very welcome! Much love to you.

7. Is This All There Is?

YES!

This Is It. As This Is. And Is Not.

But wait there's LESS

What IS this IS about which thou rantest?

Good question.

What IS "is"?

Exactly

Do You Exist?

How would you KNOW?

Heart is where the Home is.

Nobody Knows This.

Everything IS This.

ASKING…

WHO? For WHAT!?

Nothing.

How Do I Know I Exist?

How Do I Know YOU Exist?

How do YOU know I Exist?

Huh!?

Just Ask You

AM I?

….. How do I know I exist?

8. The Addict You Believe You Are

What are the Core Addictions?

Isn't it to I / Other?

Is it that this "I" seems to think, "I think therefore I am"?

The knowing naturally is I AM. I exist.

Yes?

I am. YES.

I am 'me'. Really? And what exactly is a 'me'??

Ask YOU:

Did I used to believe this nonsensical uncomfirmable noise that claims in deep space like a matrix, "I think therefore I am"? Or even more new-agey, "I FEEL there for I am"?

Where's your evidence?

Who thinks "I think I exist"?

Is it that you I Know "I Exist?"

Who Knows?

Who said That!! ??

Seek the Source of these movements …..

………and see what you find…

(if anything)

9. Catch And Release

Who Can 'Accept What Comes'?

Some make claims like "We must let all possibilities exist in Peace, meaning that we accept whatever comes." Who is there to "do" this acceptance"? The undeniable FACT of The Eternal State is that all "possibilities" ARE (Already Always!) existing Here and Now in Perfect Peace.

All there IS is THAT - What-You-Are ... <u>Nondual</u> Being-Awareness-Love. Loving all that appears without a separate Love-ER!

What IS IS and prior to appearances, while permeating the appearances as Essence of All, and This ever-IS abides Beyond this false "reality" of a "we" described in that assertion.

In That which IS there IS no "we", no "person" or "persons", to "let all exist." That is arrogant ignorance. What some call "ego."

WHAT IS EGO? A thought of claiming itself to be the source of the being, doing and having of a body, mind, spirit conglomerate which on investigation can be discovered to have no independent power or will of "its" own.

This is a teaching of nice looking ignorance that can keep the seeker stuck in a false identity that continually "tries to accept" what IS - and always fails! But ONLY always......

It is quite a familiar trap. Don't get caught in that. It's like icing on a cow pie. As one guy who writes about what is real puts it, "If you think you're enlightened, throw it away and begin again. The idea of 'enlightenment' is like a big ugly monster with a pretty face, inside you. Like the idea of the Abyss is a big warm openhearted angel with an ugly face". *(From the book "Noticing What You Already Know" by Robin Dale http://nonduality.com/robindale.htm).*

The recognition of this witnessing presence is not something to be practised by an apparent separate entity. It is the impersonal recognition of and by the ever-present One-Self-Aware-Reality.

-Leo Hartong

10. Source

Where IS "the Source"?

WHAT "Source"?

IS there such a thing as a "Source"?

If so exactly WHERE IS this "Source?"

Some teachings will tell you, "YOU are the Source of who you are being, what you do, and what you have".

Others will tell you, "YOU are NOT the Source of who you are, what you do and what you have".

Which is true?

NEITHER ONE?!

Or BOTH!?

Choose your poison!

Now if you look for the source of who you are, what you think, what you feel, what you know, what you don't know, and all the rest of (ALL the rest of Totality) what do you find?

Do you find any locatable reference point that can be seen as Source?

If NOT: what is this notion of Source and either being Source or NOT being source? Is it anything more substantial than a movement of energy arises as a thought in the brain?

Look for yourself. Don't believe, disbelieve, accept, or deny any concept.

This is not about taking on beliefs of any sort; this is pointing to the actual absence of a believer-entity that assumes IT is real and then figures IT must "find the right teaching".

You must look into this for yourself. This is a matter NOT for philosophy, and NOT for belief or dogma, but rather it is a pointing to support YOU in seeing the facts of what is Real (You ARE) and what is False (the idea of a separate entity that can control and manage its dream life).

11. WHO?

Who thinks I am?

What thinks "I Think"?

Is the thought I exist always happening?

Or Not?

Can a thought think!!??

Really? Who thinks so?

Thoughts about thoughts about thoughts

Thoughts come and go.

YOU are that Eternal Love . . . .

IN which all arises, hangs about for a bit, and disappears.

What Never Changes?

YOU.

All is Perfect in The Unborn

That is here always forever now right before the next thought.

Silent Screen …

Made Of Love

12. Who knows?

"The Shadow Knows" – Really?

"Me and my Shadow" … are WE really really real?

Who Cares? "I" Care! (Who…?)

Where's the knower … claiming "I know this or that"?

Seek that.

Find that knower.

Really look into YOU for that knower, that author of the life story, the claimer of the happening of the appearing universal show as "mine?"

What is seen on looking?

Looking into naked Awareness from naked Awareness, the seeing arises for no-one that what we call "mind" is a transparency that the Light of This Loving Isness shines through, creating the show, just like the light in the movie projector seems to make the movie appear on a blank white empty ordinary screen.....

Being Is Primal and prior to States Of.

The issue of your fundamental identity goes right to the heart of discovering your essential nature of non-conceptual awareness (many terms are used to point to it). In realizing your real identity, there is a simultaneous understanding of the nature of appearances, since they are only an expression of that which you are. In that non-conceptual reality, there is no concept present of an "I", "you", "other" and so on, as all those notions are created in thoughts, which are a subsequent appearance on the pure awareness itself.

-John Wheeler

13. Being – The Eternal State

What IS this "Eternal State"…?

Our website is known as TheEternalState.org.

But wait … what does that "name" point to?

Awareness and only that. Nondual, Undivided, Totality, Isness, Unicity – these are also words that point to That Which Is yet cannot be grasped. To try to grasp This with the thought-form of that which we call "the mind" is rather like trying to grasp space with your foot.

The original working title of "Paradise Found" title was "Being, the Eternal State".

But there was a nagging Energy from Oneness that there was still something a bit misleading in that expression. (She never lets anything that could be misleading get past Her!)

So that energy was pondered , and was found intuitively that the title as it was didn't really seem to express this wild, open, raw LOVE that in direct experience here IS the actuality of what is Real, alive and Never-ending. Then I received a contribution from a great guy who points out the Real in some of the same ways it happens here.

Here is that interchange:

What Is 'The Eternal State'?

I asked Randall Friend (a cool guy who shares this One-Essence from Kentucky, USA) – "How would you respond to a seeker who asked, 'I hear about 'the eternal state'. Sounds like freedom from fear of death amongst other 'good things'. But MY question is, What IS 'The Eternal State'?"

Randall points out,

The "Eternal State" is not really a state at all - it is THAT IN WHICH all states appear. A "state" can only be known through distinction, through using words and thoughts to define the appearance, to define the very ONE who is looking for this state; to create a story of a ME that wants some Eternal State. But words aren't the thing - words never actually break up the appearance, never actually create separation, never actually create a subject and object.

Once we speak of or try to define an Eternal State, we assume all other states and someone who can find it. The "Eternal State" is only ever THIS HERE NOW - it is the mind in which this world is created. The thought "I AM" appears in thought, then the world follows. Once the I AM comes, then everything OTHER THAN the I AM is assumed. Then we have an "outside" world in which "I" am only a small, separated part, in which "I" am afraid and "I" desire, where "I" am born and "I" will die.

THIS - HERE NOW - IS the totality of present appearance, the Wholeness, Oneness itself. The "Eternal State" requires time - THIS HERE NOW requires no time, for it is all that IS - this very instant, before, during and after thought, in which the concepts of the ME, the SEEKER and the WORLD float by like clouds in the sky. You ARE the sky AND the clouds - but we only know of "sky" and "clouds" in mind.

In the Eternal Stateless-State, there is no question of states, no question of one who is seeking the Eternal State, no question of being outside of or away from or ever finding the Eternal State. And the Eternal State is fully present HERE and NOW - it is not achievable or attainable - it is UNAVOIDABLE and INESCAPABLE - NOW! As Bob ['Sailor' Bob Adamson] says, FULL STOP!

So as thoughts and words pause, there is simple resting in pure knowing, pure experiencing, present awareness in which there is no "aware-er", in which no separation EVER existed, a resting in pure SEE-Ing in which there is no ME to rest and nothing to see.

No seeker to ask the question and no one left to respond.

Randall's pointer is perfect and VERY clear! I LOVE it. And his expression of the inexpressible "Isness" IS in perfect alignment with some ancient texts ("Upanishads") that say much the same. Maybe a more "spiritually correct" title would have been "Being - The Eternal Stateless State". Maybe. (That's how my website has been titled for over a year.) But that all feel apart as the final title came roaring out of wild raw LOVE ... Paradise Found! Unbounded unbridled lovingness that accepts any and all appearances with absolute affection and NO attachment, and NO aversion, to any of it! The Peace that gently holds in its Divine Embrace ALL of it, love and war, hatred and lust, greed and generosity, all the opposing ideas and experiences.

Bottom line is, you cannot "Attain an Eternal State". In Being, There IS NO "Eternal State". And, YOU ARE THAT Stateless State, Unborn and absolutely FREE. In That, anything can happen. Anything! Even THIS.

Again, I love what Nisargadatta said about this "state" -

"I know exactly how transient this present state of affairs is, and I also know the eternal state. I have no use for this ephemeral state. I understand the false as false. Since I have found my true permanent state I have no need for any of this; it has come on its own and it will go on its own. In that fullness there is no need of any kind. I've had that state of fullness after I met my guru; if I hadn't met him I would have lived and died as an ordinary man". *Courtesy of Pradeep Apte, aptep@yahoo.com.)*

Me too :-)... Gracias John Wheeler!

This is it. But it appears
as though it's not.
There is no individual, but
it appears as though there is.
- Jeff Foster

14. What IS "Is"?

What IS "Is?"

Asked and answered!

Resistance to what is, is suffering.

Acceptance of what is, is Peace.

So as seekers of "Truth, God, Liberation or whatever other label you like for What Is do we believe "I must NOT resist, I must accept".

Exactly WHO or WHAT will no take charge and DO this?

There is NO "path to The Truth".

There is no Truth in any path.

The Truth is This As It Is.

Right Here right Now?

No.

Prior even to that!

Then WHAT is this Isness?

NOT a concept.

NOT an experience.

NOT a perspective.

NOT a thing at all.

NOT born NOT

Yet Bodies are and die.

To take yourself to be a body that will die…

AND

To take your Self as No Thing

IS The Paradox of Everything that is No Thing.

These are NOT TWO.

Suffering is content. Awareness is context. Awareness is the source in which all arises and dissolves. Awareness remains unaffected, just like the mirror remains empty, regardless of what seems to appear in it. Recognize that you are the unaffected Awareness/Witness to which the person and its experiences – good and bad – are a witnessed object. HERE the point of gravity shifts from content to context. This context is empty and marvelous and it does not suffer. It is the peace prior to the mind generated divisions of good/bad, pain/pleasure, yin/yang. You are that Peace.

-Leo Hartong

The sage knows he doesn't exist as a separate controlling entity who can or must exercise his will to avoid 'negative' experiences and grasp onto 'positive' experiences. The sage is powerless, and he knows it.

- Stephen Wingate

15. Being Unborn

Beats The Be Jesus out of Suffering!

Just Reject The Bankrupt Paradigm Of Separation

Q: I received this message and I want to know if you agree: "When we say that God is everything, it means that HE is all that is real. What man creates through his separation-thinking and greed for power is not real. For example, Hitler created more suffering than many others dictators like him, and yet, it ended by him committing suicide and seeing how stupid the whole thing was. There was no gain it at all. He ended up like the people he treated. This doesn't mean that the war didn't happen or that people didn't suffer. It means that it was created by man's ignorance and need for personal power because they were devoid of love in their past. God had nothing to do with war and suffering in the world. God is love. Therefore anything created without love is created by man's ego. God is everything means that even Hitler has a soul that can recognize God and love but he denied through it his through his unawareness and need for lust and greed and power. God created us in His image but it is up to us what we do by our choice. God will always forgive us no matter what we do if we turn to him. God is everything means that everything has that potential of love but we have been given choice -- to choose love or fear. Of course, this choice is not conscious but unconscious mostly. Do you see that"?

Do you agree?

C. Absolutely NOT.

First off, the idea of a Big Separate God who is LOVE and therefore would never "choose war" is rampaging ignorance. If God is One and only One where is any separate ego? It's bullcrap. Look: You cannot have it both ways. Either God is ALL or God is Nothing. Where is any separate ego that can somehow "thwart" the "Will of this Loving God"?

Who chooses? That is what needs to be examined. So, NO I do not agree. There is NO ego! It's a ghost! You scare yourself telling yourself ghost stories where YOU are the main ghost character, the star in your drama. It's crap.

Don't get me in the middle between you and that writer, whom I do not know. If you keep roaming the Internet and writing to other teachers I will NOT reply to you again. As a wise man said, if you are wanting to hit water digging a well, dig in just one place. Stay with one teaching. If you like that expression what difference will my assessment make? The real question which you keep avoiding asking yourself is Who Am I"? I say refuse all thoughts except who am I? If you can, just do it. If not keep looking in all the wrong places, in thoughts and outside yourself. But get real with it, man!

In any case as I read the post it seems whoever that is, IS trying to point to the Universal I AM that we "label" God… but the idea of choice and chooser is out of ignorance. The assumption of a chooser-entity. Look for such and you simply cannot find any such thing!

So the expression is fundamentally flawed. The idea of conscious OR unconscious choice is nonsense, it depends on that ubiquitous false assumption of an "individual me", entity that has to choose to love. Who would NOT choose love if there were any real choice in the matter? The Hitler example is just silly noise.

If you stick with the final point, to refuse ALL speculations, thoughts, stories etc and come back to JUST "Who Am I"? all the questions dissolve.

Follow-up: Q: Alright, I see what you mean and I know God and I aren't separate... I just didn't get why another Advaita Vedanta teacher believed in that type of crap... Sorry, for the questions... I just want you to be my teacher

C. Be your OWN "teacher". You ARE THAT. Chooserless Choiceless Awareness. YOU ARE Just THAT. Full Stop!

That "crap" as you put it and I agree with your assessment, is the real problem when a "teacher" believes they are a "teacher-person" that is teaching "another…. a "student-person". That is a bankrupt paradigm. This that arises here and through 'Sailor'

50

Bob, John Wheeler and others in that "family" is simply, Oneness sharing Oneness with Oneness - sharing rather than teaching. The real teacher doesn't claim to know some fancy conceptual "spiritual wisdom" that you don't know and must learn. While the correct seeing is that self-ignorance is cured by Self-Knowledge THAT is the compassionate sharing of what is obvious and clear FOR YOU. That means, For who you ARE, when you look with a bit of guidance shared through one who has been down the road and knows the pitfalls and potholes and shares how to steer around them.

Stay with the Bottom Line, which you HAVE seen: You ARE That. Presence Awareness and NOTHING Else. THAT is Love. Stay PUT now, my friend.

16. What Gets Born?

And what "dies?"

"You" Die every night in "sleeping"

"You" awake every night in "Dreaming"

"You" awake every morning in the Day Dream

What IS that "you" anyway? Where are "you" right NOW?

What are you?

"I don't know really!" GOOD!

Now who is it that doesn't know?

Who?

What?

Who!

I don't know!

WHO don't know what where when?

O for heaven's sake stop already!

Have some chicken soup

Have a cookie.

For God's sake (YOUR sake) stop look listen die now be Unborn alive

Seeking Assures Never Finding.

How Is Creation Creating Itself?

Q: Just wanted to run something past you for some clarity. I was in the shower (I do my best thinking under water!) and was mulling over an interesting thought. Our whole world is based on the premise that there exists an objective reality "out there" independent of our observation. Of course, this is not provable because it is only though our thoughts and mental images that we know something. Since we're not present to hear the proverbial tree fall in the forest, it can't make a sound...independent of a "hearer."

C. Yes: Ultimately the emptiness asks WHAT tree? Your sharing is quite right as a concept that points to the non-conceptual absence of any hearer of what arises as energy and sounds like stuff heard.

Q: Isn't that true of our self as well?

C. Of course.

Q: We assume there is an "I" independent of thought just like the tree. But upon closer scrutiny, without the "I" thought...there is no "I". When "we" are absorbed in an activity, say for example, building a model airplane or playing a musical instrument...there is no "I" thought, and consequently, no "I". It's not until we "wake up" (love the paradox) and say to ourselves, "Oh, *I'm* building the model" or *"I'm* playing the musical instrument" that this "I" reappears.

C. That ain't "waking up". THAT is "going back to sleep"! But ONLY if that I is TAKEN ON BOARD as "me-apart-from-other". There is NO problem with the appearance of an I so long as that appearing and subsiding I is seen to be merely a <u>pointer</u> to what IS – the Wholeness of That which cognizes all that appears and is not actually separate from that appearance. NOT TWO.

The "I" thought is equally a manifestation of The One as is the Silence and Stillness of Emptiness all is That, <u>arising</u> as Being-Awareness-Lovingness. That Being NEVER changes. That is the TRUE <u>Eternal</u> Stateless State.

Q: It seems to me just as plausible an explanation that we (Consciousness) are creating our own reality as we observe it...millisecond by millisecond...constantly hitting the "refresh" button. And, of course, that can also be said for the mind-made "I" we also claim is objective reality. Feel free to affirm, dismantle...

C. Very accurate pointers, clearly coming from direct experiencing of the actuality of no-person. The thought I or me is NO problem so long as the thought is not believed to be what you are any longer. So in the view from Here your expression is spot on.

Ponder these pointers from "Oneness", by John Greven

Why?

Creation, the universe, is because the sense of being arose in the One. You are, for the very same reason. In this book we have talked about beingness - being what you are. There comes a time when even that pointer, that concept, can be dropped.

Consider the analogy that in sleep, prior to a dream, there is a void or emptiness – no thing. Then the dream appears. It arises spontaneously and nothing is actually happening. So it is for the One. In the beginning there was the One, at peace with itself. In the One, the sense of being arose, and just as the nightly dream spontaneously arises, so creation appears.

The One knows space, time, and creation to be unreal against the One reality which it is. As the source, the One knows itself as the sole reality even while loving the appearance of beingness. The One is loving to be, and knowing that, in truth, nothing is really happening.

To further the analogy, creation is a dream of the One and the dream is not separate from the One just as the nightly dream is not separate from the organism dreaming. Creation could come to an end at any moment and the One, that is the single reality, would remain – nothing would be missed.

Because no one is born and no one dies, just as in a nightly dream, the suffering that appears to take place within creation is not real. All the events of creation are not real. They are, as we have discussed, just appearances within the One.

… all of creation is appearance within the One. The appearance does not touch the One. The One loves to be, and so the appearance is. There is no further purpose than that. The appearance exists within the peace of the One and does not disturb that peace. You, as the person, are just an illusion or a dreamed appearance. You, the True Self, That which is present-aware, that which is the beingness, is likened to the drop in the ocean. Taste the drop and you know the taste of the whole ocean. Know the Self and you know the One for there is no difference and no separation from That.

The sense of presence, the sense of beingness arose in what you are and so follows the appearance of the person.

The peace that is the Source is your peace. The love that is the Source is your love. The timeless, spaceless, presence that is the One is you. There is nothing that the mind can say about it. There is nothing you need to do to achieve what you already are, nothing that needs to be acquired to be more of what you already are, and nothing that needs to be improved upon. For the ocean and the drop, there is nothing else. There is no separation between the drop and the ocean except in the mind.

Consider again the words from Chapter 12: "Stay with that which lovingly allows for everything to appear in peace that cannot be disturbed. Allow it to show you the depth of its void and the fullness of its emptiness."

The only thing standing in the way of clearly seeing what is being pointed to are the false ideas you have about who you are. These false ideas are easily dissolved with investigation and all that remains is the reality of the One, just as it has always been. Nothing new is added – you already are what you seek.

The Origin Of "I Am"

In the last chapter we discussed how creation came into existence. Prior to that, when in the One, the sense of being arose - with it arose the sense of "I Am." This is why your own beingness is such a clear pointer to your ultimate true nature. The sense of being is the source of the thought "I Am". The beingness that is sensed by the mind is the same beingness of the One. Some point by saying that there is only One and not even that. This is pointing to that which is the One prior to the sense of beingness. The sense of beingness is the very root cause of all appearance. The One, the Source, or God is so far removed from what the mind can conceive or perceive that even the presence of beingness is superficial and a mere enjoyment of the One.

The mind however is confused by this sense of beingness because it cannot grasp it. Because it cannot grasp it the mind chooses to ignore it or just overlooks it to the best of its ability and settles on the idea that "I Am." The thought "I Am" is only a reflection of the One's experience of itself. The mind, as we have seen, is a part of the creation that arose from the One. The mind, being dual, senses the beingness and sees the appearance of creation. In that lies the illusion of separation.

In order to break the spell of separation one only needs to realize that the concept of "me", the idea that "I Am," is just a thought pointing back to that beingness and to see that without that beingness - nothing would be. To see that even without that sense of beingness, you are.

In that presence nothing else is needed, required, wanted, or happening. In that presence, in the beingness that you are, lays the ultimate peace – you are that.

From the book "Oneness" by John Greven.

Get it at www.onenessjustthat.com

Highly recommended.

17. Did You Die?

What "died"?

What was "born"?

Is Death Real?

Q: Has anyone ever brought up death or loss of a loved one on a conference call?

C. Not specifically. Of course you'd be welcome to do so. In short, though:

In the experiencing of the life appearance, there can be a shock when an appearance disintegrates, similar to the organism's programming that experiences a shock like a "blue screen crash" on a PC while you are working. that is just another experience that comes and goes in This Timeless Presence. That happened here when NBC's "Meet The Press" moderator Tim Russert "died" suddenly.

There is nothing special or significant about any appearance - even death - in this movie show called "life" -except "thinking makes it so".

But the more salient question is, "what dies"? Only the "born" can "die". What got born there where "you" are? Only an insubstantial, essentially unreal, cloud-like thought of an "I". To take the unreal to be real brings a fear of dying and the assumption there are "others" called "loved ones" that CAN die. It's all assumed and NOT real in what IS.

See if you can find a "born entity" in the space of awareness where "you" appear to be, here and now, and as you find it's absence IN and AS the actuality of what IS – No Thing – then you can no longer assume a "born entity' that is real, I mean actually real, anywhere in "anyone" - in any organism-appearance.

"Death" is "time's mightiest illusion"!

("Time" is Life's mightiest illusion!)

The main thing to see is that there is no 'I' to either get in or out of the loop. It is also not 'your' mind it is just mind. Nor is it you that has to see this. There is just seeing without someone doing the seeing.

The hierarchical structure of our language demands there be an 'I' to do the seeing, and then it is forgotten that this 'I' itself is nothing but language/thought.

The 'I' in 'I think' has as much substance as the 'it' in 'it rains.'

-Leo Hartong

18. Much Undo About Nothing

You Cannot "Grasp" What You ARE

This "spiritual talking" is nothing but mistaking the feeling-thought story of "me" and "my life" as a "spiritual person" for the actual Endless Being of unconditioned unbounded Love that you really are. Stop seeking and here you are, whole and complete, awareness without beginning or end. Start seeking again and that seems to be masked or covered over but IS awareness actually masked? AWARENESS IS. You are That. Space-Like. Could Space grasp Space? No. Can you either grasp, or move out of, this awareness? Never. No. Not possible! Here is the final point: If ANYTHING - including these pointers - is assumed to be other than utter nonsense – then that creates a perspective that is absolute nonsense.

More Undo about No One.

There is NO "true" concept OR experience. All "teachings" are nonsense. The Real is a truthless land.

Any and all "knowledge" is absolutely NOT "it"... Full stop.

The core dilemma in life is living

under a false identity

or erroneous sense of self.

– *John Wheeler*

19. No Way In, No Way Out

You are Paradise. How are "you" gonna get OUT of Paradise (and why in Heavens Holy Name do you TRY!?)

Keep seeking Paradise. That will make it absolutely certain you will NEVER find Paradise.

Life Ain't Fair to "you"

Keep hoping you will get into Paradise (and find them thousand virgins)! Then you can survive and complain about how bloody unfair life is and go poor me why me ...I wish I was dead! Don't worry, Life will take care of that wanting too. All in good (or bad) "time" the Grandest Illusion Of Them All

Why "Me, God"?

Your mother already answered that one:

Just because.

I am the witnessing Presence, and so are you. Nothing can trouble you except your own imagination. There's nothing to avoid, nothing to attain.

There's nowhere to go, nothing to become. There is no one who can suffer. All is well.

-Stephen Wingate

20. Turn Around!

Do I Exist?

No.

Do YOU Exist?

No.

Then what IS all this world and people and wars and cars and and and and and.........???

Nothing.

Turn around! Look behind the eyes, listen behind the ears. What do you see? What do you hear?

There ain't nobody home back There which is Here.

Got it?

If You Say "I Got It", You Didn't.

T.T. Writes, My life is a nightmare. I want to commit suicide.

C. First off, if there is persistent and deep psychological suffering, please make sure there is not a physical component. If you have thoughts of suicide there may be a mechanical element ... get a good physician and/or psychiatrist (NOT a psychologist) to look at the machine and see if it has some chemical imbalance. Non-duality is NOT a substitute for proper medical assessment and care! It sounds like there may be a chemical imbalance in the brain.

Q: I really don't understand. I don't know how to understand what you all enlightened persons are saying. How to understand? Because I understand, I understood all you are saying. I understood it so damn well, but nothing happens. I had so many moments when I was saying 'OK now I Really got it '. And on those moments I am ecstatic, I am flying, I feel everything is so simple. I say 'man that was so simple! I can't believe I really got it.

C. That is a fleeting experience and NOT what is being pointed to. So long as there seems to be an "I" that "got it", it's not being seen. The I is only a conceptual pointer to empty presence and NOT a separate entity. And there are NO "enlightened persons.' There is no separate person, "enlightened" or not, in Timeless Being.

Q: But -- after a while, something happens; my mind comes and kills everything. Again suffering. And I get discouraged. So if I understand it so well, where is the problem? ?????   There is something I don't get! Don't tell me there isn't. There is something you understood and I don't. What is that something?

C. In the Nondual "Understanding", ALL there is to "get" is that WHO YOU ARE IS NOT A THING THAT THE MIND CAN GRASP. Yet, YOU ARE. Undeniably YOU ARE. This which you know as I AM is your true nature and THAT is NOT a thought, NOT a feeling, NOT a concept. That I AM is the same I AM "here" and the same I AM "there". - There is ONLY ONE Unicity, One Essence, ONE I AM I AM and THAT is what you truly are.

It goes, I AM. Just That and nothing else. I AM THAT I AM. That Is All.

Ask YOU, WHAT am I? NO answer is valid! NONE! YOU ARE NOT a thing the mind can grasp and own. There is nothing more than that to get.

What AM I? In TRUTH, I Do Not Know.

Or What AMI? Not That Not That Not That Not That Not That Not That Not That Not That Not That !!!!!!!!!!!!!!

THAT is LOVE. That LOVE IS YOU. Only That.

21. Paradise Found!

Where? Here. When? Now. By whom? No one. AKA You.

Really? Yes.

REALLY?

No.

What's THAT mean?

Nuttin what's So Ever

The effort to end suffering is

the very thing that sustains it.

– John Astin

~

So it seems.

But only so it seems.

-From I Am To I Am

22. You Can't Own Paradise!

What!?

You heard me!

"You" cannot OWN Paradise. YOU IS PARADISE.

Who on earth in heaven doesn't see hear know THAT?

Find that one. When you find out there is no one to own Paradise … That Is Paradise.

Ya caint git Here from Here. (Okie Wisdom)

23. Betting The Rent

Only a stupid dang FOOL would give up everything she is for no thing what so ever.

Only that same FOOL will ever regain the Paradise she never lost!

That is like betting the rent on a game fixed against your bet. Ya can't ever win not ever no!

So the bad news is, "you" cannot bet the rent to regain Paradise. What tells you "you can become whole and complete someday" is a master con man or woman. What is needed is "The Sting".

Stinging the con is the Grace of this seeing.

So: The GOOD news is, "you" cannot bet the rent to regain Paradise.

Why!? I hear the mind wail…

Cuz there ain't no such thing as "you".

So what makes you keep trying?

Who asks this! Who answers this?

24. Your Loss is The Only Gain

The Man said, "Die before ya die. Then do whatever you like. It's all good". A dude named Bankei. Very cool old dude. Gotta be 1200 years old Now and Here He IS, still yakking it up all over His Own Creation!

YOUR creation.

Die Now. When else can ya? Only Now. Body lives as you die

cuz you was never born bubba!

Dead men Talking!

Here's Jeff Foster…

A Dead Man writing…

Upon death only the story of "me" is lost. Only the story of an individual dies, and what remains was never born in the first place". – "Beyond Awakening"

On Asking "you" WHO AM I? …..

John Astin writes, When the mind is presented with the question 'Who Am I'?, the tendency is to think that there must be an answer. However, this particular question is not intended to give an answer, but to reveal that there are no answers, to point to the reality that there is nothing that you are, and nothing that you are not.

~

Write ON!

But *Wait*

There's LESS

Who asks "Who Am I"?

Without a questioner where is a question?

Without a question where is a questioner?

Ponderations!

- From I Am to I Am

25. You LOVE You!

Don't lie about it.

You LOVE to BE.

Don't kid yourself.

But wait there's less!

If YOU are "some thing" you can only love "other some things". And all too many other some things make that damn difficult! Have you noticed? If not have a go at loving that killer on death row who raped, tortured and murdered an innocent child.

NO one could possibly love that murdering scumbag.

Only no one.

Only Nothing could love it ALL. Because why? Because only nothing IS it all. Beyond two there is The One I Love and even less than that.

THAT is Love-Beyond-A-Second.

Here's Stephen Wingate, who is Nothing But Love, just like the REAL YOU, writing…

"You are seeking love, peace and the sense that everything is okay. So you come back to this. I am aware right now. I am the peace. I am the love. I am the sense that everything is okay. It's what I am. It's what awareness is—unconditional love."

Where Is Paradise Found?

26. Want To Survive and Suffer?

'S up to you

You can survive as "an individual." No problem, that's easy. Just resist This Message. Just refuse to look.

Resist what is and you stay separate.

Love what IS and you stay separate!

You can't WIN.

So what makes you keep trying?

Find that one … if you can.

So it's easy to survive as an individual. Easy as resisting what is. That's REAL easy – you already do that all the time anyway!

Agree or disagree, neither one matters a bit.

You survive as a fake by resisting What Is. Resisting being nothing.

You claim to long or Paradise. YOU are a LIAR!

27. Liar Liar Pants On Fire!

Let The Is burn out the Isn't. You isn't. what you (innocently yet ignorantly) <u>assume</u> you KNOW "you" is! But it's not your fault. There ain't no you! Nobody programmed nobody to be somebody. It seems like it happened. But where are "you"? Nowhere. A memory! Is the memory of you YOU? How can that be true? Is a memory more than words and pictures? You are the screen, not the show!

Only Love Is Real.

Who doesn't know this?

This is the Open Secret that Nobody Knows!

That Secret Love will Burn you Alive.

Burn Baby Burn!

28. What Is Knowing? Ignorance!

Ignorance Is Suffering ~ Not Knowing Is Bliss

Q: It seems that there are "jumpy shifts" from being aware of awareness, and pretending to be "me". The fundamental illusion seems to be intact; I usually believe I am "me." I don't even know what I want to say, or what the point of asking more questions is. It seems irrelevant to continue searching, pondering, and speculating. The thought "how do I end my suffering," comes in a lot, and is often believed in.

C. BY WHOM? LOOK! Where is that "I"? That comes and goes. That is easy to see! ONLY what NEVER changes EVER is REAL. Stop telling yourself these bullshit stories, man!

STOP telling this story!

Q: Even the notion of "I am me, I am me," plays over and over, causing considerable emotional upset. As you said before, I am a hopeless case, and I can't get *it*

C. Please do NOT believe that! These words are only pointers and NOT some "truth". LOOK! When you REALLY get that you cannot get it, you got it. It' just an energy of aliveness, appearing as this false sense of "me" that thinks, feels and knows "there is something I must get."

There is only what IS and that is NOT a "thing" that you can grasp, attain, own. It is too simple for the mind that wants to own everything, including Empty Meaningless Awareness. But THAT is NOT a thing! You suffer because you turn words into things and assume you know they are really REAL. That is ignorance.

You Are NOT Who You Know Yourself To Be. REALLY … You are NOT!

You assume you are the thought "me"? Where do thoughts come from? Where do they go? Are they actually "things" or merely "labels"? And what is That IN which the appearance and dissolution of all thought happens? NOTICE: There is, wherever "you" are, unmistakable and inescapable Awareness. Being, Awareness, is the Space in which thoughts arise, including the thought of a "me" that says "this is my being, my awareness". But Awareness is here always, whether the thought of "me" or "mine" is present or not! YOU are not a thought; YOU are that Space of Awareness wherein thoughts appear.

Abandon ALL "knowing". Freedom, Love and Peace consist ONLY IN NOT KNOWING.

Ponder THIS and STOP with the believing that you are a storyteller doing all that story-telling:

"Reality must always be real. It has no names or forms but is what underlies them. It underlies all limitations, being itself limitless. It is not bound in any way. It underlies unrealities, being itself Real. It is that which is. It is as it is. It transcends speech and is beyond description(s) such as being or non-being". - *Sri Ramana Maharshi*

Let the stories and the false idea that you are a word just BE. Then they'll let YOU BE -- as You Are -- Being, just That.

Full Stop!!!!!

29. Bang Bang

Big Banging Life – Nothing Special, Everything loving Itself so Up It Shows to gaze at its own reflection....

Smashing Mirrors tinkle gladly

Don't Listen To False Gurus

Q: I have heard some of your messages and I understand it pretty well intellectually at best. The reason I am writing you is because even though I have understood the theoretical part of Advaita or Non Duality, I have not been able to shake off my egotistical me so to speak. It is all theory and no practical leap in my case. My so called "me" or "separate person" is very much alive and kicking much to my dismay. (Sounds like a paradox, I know) My ego is intact and refusing to disappear. That is, my ego or separate identity is refusing to disappear or die.

C. You know! THAT is the core issue. DROP all your knowing. The only true thing the ego-mind can really assert is I DO NOT KNOW.

Q: I had met a Guru in 1997 and he said that without Guru's Grace or Destiny's hand my case was hopeless and I would have to take many more births and suffer.

C. Oh dear God! THAT is a real load of ignorant bullshit! Don't listen to these fakes! NO true teacher or teaching would lay that trip on you! It is total CRAP.

Q: I am fully aware that I have to lose my personality, individuality, or my ego-self in order to see MYSELF in my natural state.

C. Totally false. You cannot SEE "yourself". That is ignorance, dualism, the idea of being separate and having to attain your self. You ARE the Self.

Q: But my thinking machine is over active all the time without a stop. I have never stopped thinking ever in my life. Even in sleep I dream constantly and even think like I do in the daytime. I have never had sleep without dreams or deep sleep. But

77

sometimes when I am sleeping and dreaming I know that I am dreaming but the dreaming continues.

C. WHOSE "thinking machine"? What do you take yourself to be? A thought machine? Or "the thinker" called "me"? Look! You go on telling your self "I am me" and wonder why you suffer! That false identity, merely a thought that comes and goes in Awareness, which, when taken to be "you" and separated from Awareness (a foolish assumption, that!), is the root cause of your confusion and your suffering.

Q: But I am and have always been interested in Advaita. I started reading Sri Ramakrishna, Ramana Maharshi, Nisargadatta and others at around age 17 onward. But it all seems to no avail. I am unable to shed my ego, my personality, my separate identity.

C. WHO wants to shed WHAT? It's all your own imagination. All your problems are totally false, imagination only. WHO assumes you are this thought of me myself I?

Q: Ramana Maharshi says the ego or the "false thinking I" is a mysterious force that springs forth from the Real I, the SELF or Sat Chit Ananda.

C. I don't think so! This sounds like a perversion of what Ramana actually said, which was: "What is called 'mind' is a wondrous power residing in the Self. It causes all thoughts to arise. Apart from thoughts, there is no such thing as mind". If you want to study Ramana read it accurately! It is public domain, searchable on then Internet. Here is what he pointed out:

"What is called 'mind' is a wondrous power residing in the Self. It causes all thoughts to arise. Apart from thoughts, there is no such thing as mind. Therefore, thought is the nature of mind. Apart from thoughts, there is no independent entity called the world. In deep sleep there are no thoughts, and there is no world. In the states of waking and dream, there are thoughts, and there is a world also. Just as the spider emits the thread (of the web) out of itself and again withdraws it into itself, likewise the mind projects the world out of itself and again resolves it into itself. When the mind comes out of the Self, the world

78

appears. Therefore, when the world appears (to be real), the Self does not appear; and when the Self appears (shines) the world does not appear. When one persistently inquires into the nature of the mind, the mind will end leaving the Self (as the residue). What is referred to as the Self is the Atman. The mind always exists only in dependence on something gross; it cannot stay alone. It is the mind that is called the subtle body or the soul (jiva)".

The solution is stunningly simple: Ramana said, "The thought 'Who am I?' will destroy all other thoughts, and like the stick used for stirring the burning pyre, it will itself in the end get destroyed. Then, there will arise Self-realization".

THIS is one possible pointer: Refuse ALL questions, assumptions and thoughts of me or I and ONLY maintain that one final thought, "Who Am I?". DO NOT ANSWER. Come back to the one erasing thought, "Who Am I?". Get busy on THAT. The ball as always is in YOUR court. There comes guidance but YOU must take the action to dissolve the false.

Q: You say it is a non entity, a fiction. But this non entity or fiction is making me NOT see my true nature which you have said is Sat Chit Ananda.

C. I do NOT say to BELIEVE ANY of that! That is a prompt, a pointer, and what is always said is you MUST investigate for yourself! Believe NOTHING!

Q: But no matter what, my ego does not want to die. Or should I say that I am refusing to die. Me or my ego continues to play this mischief. It seems useless and I feel sick to my stomach when I see all the tapes of you and others and I am unable to erase the separate identity and see myself as just the Real "I am, I am". You may say the ego is simply not there but I feel it is there. I am not a full time seeker like many others. But I feel just reading Advaita and not living and breathing Advaita is hypocritical. I am fully aware that I have to lose myself or die in order to see MYSELF. But I am unable to do so.

C. WHO claims all these limitations!? Arguing for your limits is an exercise in absolute ignorant futility. Go back to what Ramana told you to do!

79

Read the pointers on the website. DO what is pointed out to take action on. You are NOT a helpless little victim of some imagined destiny! Come back to simply this:

The I AM that You are is certain. WHAT you are is NOT a thing that can be described, attained, or held onto. Look for a separate entity and you will find nothing. You are That – No Thing. Follow the pointers and DO what is offered. It is up to you and you alone.

Ponder this:

"Looking for the cause of the ego is a fool's errand. The ego is an erroneous belief. The assumed ego is not present on direct investigation. Is it reasonable to search for the cause of something that is not there?"

- John Wheeler

30. Gifts Of One for One

Notice that the ego is taken to be a "fact" where it is only an assumption of a belief in something unreal. This so-called "ego" is a fantasy, and that is NOT real to begin with! Then all manner of practices are "prescribed" to annihilate this fantasy of a false ego. But since the practices assume the fact of an ego and thereby only reinforce the illusion, how could they take the ego beyond itself? It's a totally false assumption, a faulty premise, operating unnoticed in the background of all that story of practices leading to perfection "someday!" Where IS this ego? Can you find one anywhere? Apart from a simple one-letter thought ... "I" ... which is merely a cloud-like appearance assumed in ignorance to be a thing apart from the whole, there is NO ego, and NO separation, only an IDEA of such. Can an idea, a thought, separate itself from the aliveness, awareness, in which it arises? And what is at work here that is driving the appearing thoughts of "me and the universe?" Where is a me apart from that infinite Energy that drives totality to appear as manifestation and seeming (ONLY seeming!) separate objects and separate pseudo subjects? Subject/Object ... "I/Other" ... IS the core delusion.

31. "Facts" are Fiction

She who knows, Knows not. But wait!

Nobody knows that. That would be more-better-different "spiritual" knowing. Where IS the "knower"?

Who knows?

Not even "God" knows that.

Find out where the knower is and you laugh till you're silly.

Just The Fact, Ma'am

As both John Adams and Ronald Reagan once said, "Facts are stubborn things". What is the ONE indisputable FACT that cannot be argued or denied? You ARE. That Being-Knowing, I AM, is the absolute and only FACT that you can never dispute! To be as you are is effortless and unavoidable. That I AM here and that I AM there are NOT "two I Am's". So stick with the fact - and only the fact - of your Being. This is the effortless Living Reality, Living Freedom. I AM and That Is All.

32. Fact IS Fiction. Hello?

Is You Is

Or Is You Ain't?

Oh baby!

Is you is or is you ain't?

Good question.

If the mind answers ignore it. It ignores Your Essence of Being. Give it a taste of its own poison. Just ignore the liar and ask you for the absolute answer, from The One You Are and NOT that thinking-machinery that erupts in energy vibrating and making Brain Farts. Too many thought-beans. Blat!

Brain farts.

What IS the answer? WHO asks?

What asks? What answers? No such thing, ya see? There is NO answer.

There you have it!

Here you ARE It.

Facts are stubborn things.

– USA's 2nd President John Adams

The fact of your being is evident and beyond any doubt. So just have a direct look into this and make sure what you are is clear. If you keep your investigation directed to the core question and get that resolved, you will find there are few, if any, other issues that remain to be resolved.

"What you are cannot be known as an object. But still your actual presence is not absent. Although what you are cannot be known, neither can it be unknown. Beyond the known and unknown is undeniable being-awareness, utterly undisturbed and free of duality.

– John Wheeler

You cannot say, "I am not". Even in sleep, no one will deny their being either. This being or presence (whatever it may be called!) is what is being pointed to as your abiding nature.

– John Wheeler

33. Lucky YOU. You found Paradise!

Or did you?

If you find it you can lose it. If you lose it you can find it. If you want to keep suffering claim EITHER finding OR losing Paradise.

LOOK!

You ARE Paradise. To seek it is to lose it. Don't be loser OR a finder.

Just BE. Full Stop.

Could that could be simpler?

BE. No Way Out. BE. That is Paradise Found … by No-one!

Return To I Am …

J.B. Writes to follow up: Good Morning, Charlie; I just wanted to thank you for a few things: 1) The ton of non-dual bricks that got dropped on my head a week or two ago has been good for me. Things seem to be getting simpler. [I realized] The thoughts and feelings—pay them no mind, J.B. Same goes for the questions. [JB continues] I say to that mind … Don't get identified with any of it, return to the I am, and when the identification amps up, just ask the question (check out the who of it), grace allowing. Just relax, J., it's out of your hands.

He goes on to say, 2) The other thing I'm thankful for is the one-pointed, non-stop thrust that seems to come through you in every direction (books, blogs, YouTube, calls). I can, for example, open up a copy of the book " No Way Out", and turn to any page and any sentence on that page "hits the nail on the head" as my dad used to say. No distractions, no fluff, no B.S.! Undiluted, it seems.

He continues, No it's not you doing it and if it's all one – so who am I going to be thankful to? Maybe rather than I'm thankful to, it's —just gratitude and a sense of love and relief that things are in some way on track— I do keep reading non-dual passages and in some way the passages seem to confirm what's already percolating. For some reason, there's still seems a need to read the exact same thing, said a million different ways, so that it gets crystal clear. Maybe that's overkill, left over from the days of a dad who couldn't stop saying, "You've got to do better"? Take care / /thanks / Love!

C. Excellent news!

I am happy to hear this. Your great Heart is clear and present all ways, here and now.

Much Love to I AM called JB from I AM called charlie!

34. Seeing

I see said the blind man.

I hear said the deaf woman. I am said the child of a barren woman.

The One seeing is not you.

The One hearing is not you.

I know that, says the village idiot.

No, says the One. There is knowing and no I knower not not not stop NOW.

Is There Really a "Someone Looking Out"?

Q: When looking at the mind with "everyday" or "naked awareness" there is the noticing that there is no one looking and nothing but dark, emptiness to "see". It feels natural, but is eventually the space is filled by thoughts. Some still grab away attention, and the "noticing of noticing" stops. When looking out at the world, there is again the sense that there is someone looking out, although "he" cannot be found.

C. If the person cannot be found is it real? No. So why continue to invest any energy into believing that that there is an actual "someone looking out"?

Q: The question "do I exist?" is answered with a resounding "emptiness". I am the no-thing that notices that silence, that is aware of even being conscious... but this too, is clouded over in everyday life by everyday events. Sometimes there is "me-ing" and other times there is the noticing of things being done effortlessly by the body, with no one doing it.

C. Existence is and knows itself as being awareness. Conscious Presence – I AM - is Real. And all that you describe including the story of a "someone looking out" arises IN that.

Q. Life is still happening as it did before. There is no longer what you called the "Advaita buzz". There is certainly no constant bliss, but there is much less suffering. Anger and imaginary "slights" don't stick and are quickly forgotten.

C. That is the fruit of the clear seeing.

Q: What is troubling (I know, to whom?) is that unless the pointers are frequently reviewed, and the focus changes, (although this no-thing that I am continues to notice and allow as always), the old ghost of "me" seems to arise, and thinking that it is in charge, soon steals the show.

C. Does anyone truly exist that actually "steals the show"? Is there really a me that needs to continually review? NO. this residual belief can come and go for "awhile" but so long as you don't believe the story being told by the mechanistic mind, there is no real issue here.

Q: Is there still, perhaps a "me" here trying to be an "Enlightened Person"?

C. Only in a story that is told by a non-existent entity not fully seen AS non-existent! The way I see this, there is no real problem with any of the above apart from a sticky belief in an entity with control, which needs seeing that it's an unreal assumption and nothing substantial or real. Start from the I AM that You are in reality: Empty Being filled with the transcendent Light of Conscious Presence bubbling out as unavoidable waking aliveness. That is the Real. Then notice all the stories the thought machine tells and simply refuse to believe that there is any "someone". There is NO problem with a thought of being someone. Only do not believe the thought to be who you are! It's that simple.

35. I AM

I am complete – I am not complete.

WHO?

A brief chat with the One from the One:

What IS The "I" Really?

The I is an imaginary character you have assumed is the real you only in innocence. It's like you believe in Santa Claus. The tooth fairy. The "I" - me. You must give up all childish beliefs. These "entities" including the so-called "me-entity", the core misunderstanding which arrived at around age two, are ALL fictional. That primordial illusion that all the rest depend on, this "I" idea, was the first to come and is nearly always the last to go. The fictional "me", is always the last illusion to be disillusioned of!

That "I" simply needs to be seen and understood for what it is … nothing but a thought with no substantiality … just bubbling energy arising in Timeless Awareness. Yet YOU ARE so that "I" MUST represent something. It does! The sound "I" POINTS to awareness, which is always so and prior to time and thought. That is always here now wherever you are and whatever you think. Stop searching and there You are, simple awareness, free and clear. This is The Eternal Is and all your problems are completely imaginary. All is taken care of. You need not meddle with Nature. She brings the organism everything it needs when it needs it. It could NOT be otherwise. Trust THAT.

YOU ARE AWARENESS, NOT the "thought-story", the imaginary waking-dream character which appears and disappears in thought. All the time you take your actual being to be this thought you try to get that thought back to wholeness, which just reinforces the sense of being a thing apart from other things and from "God" or The One.

There are NOT "two I Am's" - I AM is universal, singular. That is The Timeless One which YOU know as your sense of being … your very Is-ness … the knowing YES I AM … but that sense of Being is neither thought nor feeling. It is simply awareness. Just that! It's this serene, blank, accepting, empty space of knowing, I AM which encompasses all that appears within it in unconditioned, Infinite, Impersonal Love. You are Love. Nothing more, nothing less!

Naturally you do know that YOU ARE. That is NO Thing. Know yourself this way: "That, I Am". "I Am That". This is the ancient pointer to what You are, NOW, Here, Eternally. Just This and NO other! This is "Advaita" – "Not Two." NON duality.

Without taking a thought, and considering a thought to be what you are, where any is separate "you" that is not surrendered to a separate "God?" Who would surrender to whom?? A thought? Can a thought do ANYTHING? It's just a thought that comes and goes in awareness. You are that Awareness, NOT that thought. This I-apart from other - and God - is a story of suffering. Look for the one telling the story. Do you find any separate thing apart from thoughts about thoughts? A vicious circle of falsehoods? To say it as directly as can be noted in language: There IS No God and YOU Are God. Sit with that, like you're letting a pillow rest in your lap.

Look at it this way:

"'I am' itself is God. The seeking itself is God. In seeking you discover that you are neither the body nor the mind, and the love of the self in you is for the self in all. The two are one. The consciousness in you and the consciousness in me, apparently two, really one, seek unity and that is love." – *Sri Nisargadatta Maharaj (courtesy of Pradeep Apte, aptep@yahoo.com.)*

There was never any separation. You have a concept "I" or "me" and another concept "God". But God, or "The Absolute", is already HERE NOW as your own sense of being, I AM. As the truth is told in language, "God" is defined as "I AM THAT I AM." You cannot separate yourself from what you are.

36. It's SO Unreal - Really?

"Reality But Really - Reality"

Existence and Nothingness: Being

– by Chad Barber (www.strangeflesh.net)

When it is noticed in your own direct experience that this luminous-living-nowness is in fact empty of any self-nature or 'thingness', it appears to be that nothingness is living as you.

Yet, there is an aspect of 'is-ness', or existence, too. There is someone existing, but at the same time it is no-thing at all. This seemingly contradictory play between existence and nothing correspondingly characterises what the unfolding of this insight feels like for us as ordinary human beings. On the one hand, it is seen clearly that there is no-one in control and that there is no-one, anywhere who is doing anything – everything is an expression of Reality spontaneously unfolding. On the other, there is a sense of a particulate self, a person going about his or her life, doing, talking and feeling.

It is this, apparently, paradoxical perception that the conceptual mind has trouble digesting. How do we deal with being someone, yet in fact no-one at all? Surely, the mind thinks, it is one or the other? Fortunately it does not have to be grasped by the mind for it to take place. It is happening all the time, and will continue to happen. The play between existence and nothingness is how Reality is 'real-ing' itself.

Existence in this sense is a direct and immediate expression of nothingness or emptiness -the two are inseparable. Is it possible to separate the objects of awareness from awareness itself?

When looking at thoughts, for instance, we see that there is a thought that arises and then it is gone again, then another arises and it is gone. It happens spontaneously without any effort. There is living-nothingness and then an object arises out of it (existing) and then it disappears again. This happens on every level; a kind of dance appears to be going on. We could call this play between existence and nothingness be-ing, or Being. This movement is spontaneous and self-perfected.

It is possible to relax into this spontaneous, effortless, and natural way of being. It is an undercurrent of peace and wholeness which we can notice to be intrinsic. It is this simple sense of being that we have all day long. And this sense of being is a natural expression this play between existence and nothingness, or emptiness, which is why when we notice it and relax into it there is a sense of spaciousness and clarity. It is very vivid and real, yet also very simple and uncontrived. It is often described as the natural state, because it is the natural basis for all our experiencing and feeling. What feelings, perceptions and thoughts can happen but in this present moment of being?

This present moment of being is the foundation, and we can feel into it right now. It only has to be noticed – not created, or sustained. It has flavour of silence, presence and nowness – these words are only clues, which can hopefully trigger recognition when it is seen in your own direct experience.

When it is apprehended clearly, you will see how it is possible to be both agitated and peaceful at the same time, or sad and peaceful, or even peaceful and peaceful. The undercurrent of peace that we are talking about is so basic, so simple, that it cannot be disturbed or clouded by temporary emotional responses. It is the foundation of the spontaneous happening that you know as yourself. Everything is an expression of this basic peace.

37. Beyond Reality, Beyond 'I Am'

Q: Whatever it was that woke me is now downloading more of your audio sessions to take to the gym on my portable audio player. From there What will run the legs, lift the weights and reason that all the sweat is being done for the chocolate smoothie at the imagined end. ha ha ha

C. What indeed? Good question. <u>No</u> answer will capture or evoke The Real beyond reality!

Q: I am"... the day... Silence pretending to be M.

C. Potent Pointer from Sri Nisargadatta Maharaj:

"This primary concept, 'I am-ness' is dishonest, because it is still a concept only. Finally one has to transcend that also and be in the 'nirvikalpa' state, which means the concept-free state. Then you have no concept at all, not even of 'I am'. In that state one does not know that one is. This state is known as 'Parabrahman': 'Brahman' transcended. 'Brahman' is manifest; 'Parabrahman' is beyond that, prior to that; the Absolute". *Sri Nisargadatta Maharaj (courtesy of Pradeep Apte, aptep@yahoo.com.)*

Beyond Reality You Are - Subjectless Objectless Just One.

No-one knows That.

Love Ya!

Your spiritual search is a joke. You will never attain freedom from the I-concept. You will never attain enlightenment. You are the watching so just watch.

– Stephen Wingate

38. <u>This</u> IS Paradise

If you seek it you lose it. LET GO.

(Now who is here to let go!?) Ha!

The Two-Sided Coin of "Nonduality"

Q: A few days ago I chanced on a segment of yours on YouTube. I found it interesting and articulate. I then checked out a few others and recently even ordered a CD set from your web site. What you say (along with many others who provide pointers to the truth of Advaita), however, tends to down play one thing. Everyone says, "All things appear in awareness... Awareness has no beginning and no end...You are it. Nothing new is to be attained...You have always had it and that is what you are... So there is no such thing as enlightenment... etc."

C. That is not what the whole sharing is. We do point out the inescapable Awareness that is always present, right here, right now. But unlike some who ONLY point to That and affirm You Are That, we recognize here that for many seekers there are seeming obstacles in the mind that must be addressed, seen, challenged and dissolved. The happening here is to provide BOTH SIDES of the Nondual Coin, so to speak. A one sided teaching will rarely suffice. There are exceptions but they ARE few and far between!

Q: Now I can see that everything I perceive appears in awareness. Thoughts and emotions arise and subside in it, etc. But this is still a far cry from knowing *through the immediacy of experience* that awareness is everything, that all things are derived and are dependent on awareness. Having an intellectual conviction of it does not do much for me.

C. For WHOM? Is there a "me" assumed, an "I" apart from The All?

Q: I is obviously the *experiential* realization that the ego is a false entity that releases me into the freedom that I supposedly am. Instead of harping on the fact that we are already That, I feel it would be useful if teachers or commentators on nonduality spent more time on *how* to make that truth the stuff of experience.

C. I basically agree! To see that the "I" is a POINTER to Timeless Being and NOT a "thing apart" is realization - for no-person. But if that isn't seen, then this is why when the seeker is really ready to tackle his or her false assumptions, after pointing out the brilliant obviousness of being, always present and aware as the silent screen on which all appears, we say IF you still believe there is separation, an entity apart from the Whole that assumes IT is in charge and must manage its life and also somehow manage to "get enlightened," to follow a simple pointer:

I sometimes say refuse all thoughts except "who am I?"! No matter how much it's stressed it often goes unheeded - as seekers stubbornly want an answer to that rather than simply ask, refuse all answers, and stop in silence. That Silence IS what all beings ARE and that final unanswered question there is the possibility for realization, right here right now! And, quoting Sri Ramana Maharshi: "The thought 'who am I?' will destroy all other thoughts, and like the stick used for stirring the burning pyre, it will itself in the end get destroyed. Then, there will arise Self-realization".

This IS repeated over and over until it finally sinks in! I have been taken to task by some who reject this as "merely reinforcing the egoic sense of a separate self", but I speak from my direct experience only in sharing what simply works and has passed the test of time. The pointers on how to investigate - to root out the false core belief in "me", "time", and " separateness" – which IS what some call "ego" – come from the ancients and were embraced and taught by REAL Sages whose gifts endure because – THEY WORK! Who cares whether a teaching or one who shares their experience of being free fits some established dogma? Or some NEW dogma!? Both sides of that silly argument over "neo-Advaita" and traditional-Advaita" are simply an ignorance of often unobserved dualism! These sorts of things do propagate suffering. Far more powerful is to inquire into WHO believes all these lies of mind and ego? WHO AM I? Is the stunningly SIMPLE means.

Q: It is true there is a danger that any practice can be converted into a lifeless ritual. But absence of any practice also keeps one mired in a life of selfhood. (In fact, it may even make some very complacent that they are already That and there is nothing left to do.) So more pointers on how to recognize "what we have always been and are" would be welcome. You might say that sages like Ramana and Nisargadatta have already dealt with this. True, but then so have they already dealt with the fact that we are That. These things could use repetition---especially from people who have realized through the techniques espoused by those sages.

C. Absolutely. No argument here. In most cases - (including my own, as John Wheeler and Bob Adamson kept after me to get down into the false to root it out) - there must be a constant prompting to return to the basics of this: 1) You already ARE what you seek, this Presence, empty and loving all that appears within it, IS your true natural stateless state, and 2) If this is not clear the investigation into the assumed self center that takes itself to be a "me-apart-from-the-One" as a habit of mistaken identity, the error of taking a thought, "I", to be real, solid and separate. Rigorous challenging of that does reveal that the assumed entity with assumed volition or control simply never did exist. It seems to take time because the habit of thinking deeply in the background "I am me" has been reinforced over years or decades since about age two. So it would be irresponsible and foolish to expect that it can be dismantled overnight (though as always there are exceptions but the vast majority of seekers of truth ARE afflicted with the virus-lime paradigm of "me-time-separation" and it must be dismantled with earnestness and commitment).

Now, will YOU abandon ALL thoughts, questions, assertions, claims, stories, and simply refuse it all and only abide in the thought-form Who am I?? Let That erase '"you"!

Q: Anyway, just a thought. With best wishes,

C. So long as you see that you are not a thought, and that You are Unborn, then all is naturally perfect – just as it is. Always was. Always shall be. Endless Beginningless Peace.

What exactly is born? What is born are three states: the
waking state, the sleep state, and the knowledge 'I am',
this consciousness. The body and the vital breath
would not be able to function if this consciousness
were not present. These three states work through the
three attributes [concepts of nature, called 'gunas' –
rajas-energy, tamas-sloth, sattva-purity]. I very clearly
see that which has been born. And I also know that I
am not that which is born. And that is why I am totally
fearless.

*- Sri Nisargadatta Maharaj (courtesy of Pradeep
Apte, aptep@yahoo.com)*

39. Nothing Happens "Next". THIS IS IT

Q: I don't really know where to start with this message! Your website and YouTube videos are so inspiring – thank you! The reason for me contacting you is really born out of frustration, and a wanting to come back home.... but deep down I know this doesn't even compute because I never left 'home' anyway! All I can say is that I have had a taste of my true nature..... And somehow, the veil came crashing back down.

C. I know that feeling well. Happened in 2002. Getting into the wedding feast then getting tossed out into the dark night, much wailing and weeping and gnashing of teeth as someone said a couple thousand years ago.

Q: I hope u can help. In February this year I suddenly found myself in what I now understand to be that stateless state. At the time I could not really qualify those wonderful 2 weeks at all.... hence, since that period I have undergone a rigorous search for answers to what happened.

C. That is definitely barking up the wrong tree! All answers are LIES. Mental understanding is the booby prize!

Q: Much reading, web-research, internal questioning has led me to this point now of teetering over the cliff edge. After reading Nisargadatta, Sailor Bob, et al..... where now? I totally 'get it' on an intellectual level....... but.... something lacking.

C. Who feels lack? What is that based on? Is there the deep assumption that 'you" are actually separated from Oneness and must somehow attain that "again"? Oneness is what you ARE and That is NOT an "experience that comes and goes". Sometimes these glimpses can be the worst thing for a seeker because these fleeting experiences, wonderful though they may SEEM to be, are a SHAM, a scam the mind uses to sucker "you" into believing "that was IT - Big Casino! - And I gotta get THAT BACK"! But THAT is the <u>absence</u> of "you". How can an ABSENCE get ABSENCE BACK??

Now, Here, either there is the apparent "presence of you" or the apparent "absence of you" but this is irrelevant to what YOU actually ARE – The Presence of Awareness that silently registers both the presence and the absence of the assumption of an entity that comes and goes like the weather.

Q: I guess I must ask: "WHO, exactly, is getting it?"

C. Good question! Ask YOU that one. Accept absolutely NO answer.

Q: All I know is that this being-ness that arose is very very REAL. So real. And so close. Closer than close. All fear disappeared; in fact, I could clearly see fear for the very hoax that it is - just a phantom! Love entered. I giggled almost constantly and uncontrollably, and kept telling my closest friends "I am in you as much as I am in myself". My eyes were glazed over, everything had a very dreamlike feel, nothing was serious, and I felt like everyone was in on the game and new all about it! I kept telling one of close friends "we're all playing Truman in the Truman show."!!! I felt that in any minute someone was going to walk in and lift the curtain and say "that's it, you've got it! Game over".

C. All lovely yet NOT what is pointed to! The telltale of the mistake is in this ignorance assuming that "*you've got it!*" ALL of that happens in this Presence, this Empty obvious Awareness that you REALLY are. And now you describe a memory as if it actually happened but that is all imagination. A story told by an imaginary entity taking itself to be real and having real experiences. All a story happening in This Now that you really are. All stories arise "once upon a time" and come and go on the silent screen of Timeless Being.

You will never be able to grasp That. You might as well try to put the sky in a bucket!

Q: I definitely felt that the game was over. Looking at faces, on TV, in papers, looked like myself looking back at me. Every time I read something I seriously felt that I already wrote it and was just reading it back to myself, as if from far away I had sent this to myself..... And yet I didn't know about it until I read it. Every moment was being drawn up, all rooms and spaces were being perpetually drafted out of nowhere.......

C. The problem is right there in that first sentence: "I" felt the game was over". That is the evidence that it is NOT. Again, all quite lovely and amazing, yet NOT what is pointed to! Again, ALL of that happens in this Presence, this Empty Obvious Awareness that you REALLY are. Wondrous though that experience seemed, it seems so to "you" and "you" do not exist. There is no "you" in This Being Loving Aliveness, the Peace that is the Real, shining before the next thought or feeling, Right Here Right Now -- allowing for the appearance of all those happenings, wondrous, horrid, whatever arises shows up and goes back into That Being which You are.

Q: The overriding theme was love.... and that love doesn't choose or discriminate.... everything was evenly coated and driven by love in equal measure...... everything worked in harmony and I could see clear relevance within everything, everything was trying to help..... Everything pointing back to itself again and again. Things worked. No obstacles. Everything felt like a variation on the same one theme. I knew this was it. And then, I fell! I 'lost' it....... even though I know, at least intellectually, it can never be lost. But still..... I misplaced that presence. So now every second of every day is a yearning for that again...... I remember knowing the moment of downfall.... it was the arrival of fear again, but fear of losing this being-ness, losing the dearest of the dear, or losing this not-knowing)....... what a wicked trick to play on myself!!! And when that fear set in the beingness started to fade away... awful. I know now that the error is in thinking that "I am"...... as, how can fear exist if there is nobody there claiming ownership of it?!!! Seems so daft. But no matter how much I convince myself of this fact, I still feel somewhat stuck. But again - WHO exactly is stuck?!!!!

C. Who is telling that story that appears in this Now that you are?

Q: So, I wonder if you can help me? Where now? Just to sit and wait? What occurs now?

C. Nothing. Nothing happens "next". THIS IS IT. You are This NOW and all that Shows Up Now. NOT TWO.

Q: Every now and again I feel as if a chink in the armour of misidentification falls away... and some more light, the Bright Light of Awareness breaks through. Just this last 15 minutes I read something in Sailor Bob's book that really REALLY hit home: "There is nobody here now, or at any other time, who can negate their beingness. No one can ever say 'I am not'". This is fairly straight forward...... what actually hit home was the internal dialogue which followed within me.

C. Again the me!? Where IS that "me"? A thought that comes and goes in Present Now Awareness. Nothing substantial. Meaningless! Utterly meaningless.

Q: And this is what I need clarification with. As a bit of background, I have been working on and looking deeply into this "I AM" for some time now. Well, after reading the above sentence in Bob's book it suddenly occurred to me that I no longer even wish to humour the thought "I AM". The reason is simple: even the thought "I AM" is an abstraction and deviation AWAY from the ONENESS. It is still a MIND translation. It, quite simply, is still not IT !!!!! Sure, it is as close as the mind can get to describing ONENESS. But still.... surely it is WAY off the map???? Right?

C. WHO wants to know? WHO claims "I" this and "I" that!? Right? NO! Wrong? NO! You are trying to parse and dissect and figure out the un figure outable.

Q: So, surely we could add to Bob's statement, the words ….

C. Don't mess with Bob's words! LOOK how they point to what is Real. All the rest of what you wrote up trying to "interpret" Bob is crap, my dear friend.

Q: And, like you said on one of your recent videos, all that can be truly said is: "EXISTENCE IS". FULL STOP. How can we possibly take it any further? I cannot..... So, its time to kick back and eat some fish and chips....

C. Excellent move! Checkmate the false mind. Time for some Sole Food, for the organism … add some Stout and have a nice long nap. Do NOT trade this Unborn Now for "time" and "separateness". Do NOT accept the bullshit story of "I and other". All there is is all there is. The One and That means The One. Even the appearance of a flip-flop in an out is also The One. Enjoy your Fish and Chips and DON'T forget the vinegar and the Stout. (Burp.)

Q: I really hope you can help.... and point me in the right direction......

C. No "you" and no "direction". No one to help no one to BE helped.

Q: You are wonderful, many thanks.

Takes One to know One. Love ya!

What is being pointed to is your natural being, which is always present and aware. You cannot understand this via the mind. It is what the mind comes and goes within. It is always present knowing and illuminating the mind. It is present when the mind is active, and it is present when it is not active. The presence or absence of the mind makes absolutely no difference to what you are.

– John Wheeler

40. Once Upon A Time …

Tell me a story, said the little one to the bigger one she calls mommy. All right said the big one called mommy, "Once upon a time Big You became a little big me called mommy and a little small you called Johnny and and and and … OH! Once upon a time, Paradise is Lost.

Paradise was Lost.

Weep and wail. Gnash Teeth. Continue forever and ever old world without end ayyeeeee man!

But then, said little big me called mommy, YOU ran out of time … just as fast as you could … because you know time was not-paradise and Timeless IS Paradise. And so little one said to the big little one called mommy, but mommy, I was never born. You are only dreaming. And big little mommy woke up and cried and laughed until time began again.

And Big You chuckled and said, now THAT was the most fun game of hide in plain sight I ever played.

…and everyone loved happily never after.

Ultimately, you have no control over the mind states, so let them be. Lose the concern that there is something significant about the mind and emotional states. They are simply passing states. End of story. They don't mean anything about you at all. As you clear up your real identity, the mind will take care of itself.

– John Wheeler

41. I Don't I Can't I Can I Won't I Will

That I, when assumed to be a "person", IS the cause of all suffering!

Drop it all and BE

"How"?

Who asks?

Question and questioner... aren't they just a partnership of assumed entitification in a thought story?

Where is the storyteller?

You ARE.

BE.

You know you are sitting here; you know you are, do you require any special effort to hold on to that 'you are'? You know you are; abide only in that. The 'I am' principle without words, that itself is the God of all 'Ishwaras' ['divine Beings'].

–Sri Nisargadatta Maharaj (courtesy of Pradeep Apte, aptep@yahoo.com.)

42. Love Rocks

Being One Letting Go of stuff you never had is FUN ain't it!

Want a new lease on Life"

Forget about it. That's so yesterday!

Hey? Don't Lease another me-life. Re-lease Life into Love.

Who Releases?

No one No thing No where No here Now Now

Wow

Loving Hate is a Hootless Hoot!

Being Love, Hate happens and so what?

Not-You LOVES LOVES LOVES to hate ... when it arises.

LOVE hate to DEATH LOL

You Is So Love-Able...

You Love I

I Love You

Same Difference

Apparently a Different Sameness

How Hot is THAT?

1000 Celsius melting no already melted the wax mask The One that The One used to call "you-me-we-them-us."

We don't need no steenkin' names!

YES, We Have No Masks Now Now

NO HERE NO NOW HA! NOW THAT IS LOVE

(So To say)

Love Abides In Not Knowing

The point is to clarify who and what you are. You exist. That is certain. What this, your present being, is, is often not clear. The method is to find out your natural and abiding nature that does not change or vary under any circumstances. Get to know the space of being-awareness — not by thinking about it, but intuitively, non-conceptually. Make friends with this. After all, it is your most intimate, abiding and natural self. Notice its presence, openness, clarity and so on.

- John Wheeler

43. Heart To Heart

A follow-up from J.B. - Deeply moved watching "Thank You, John Wheeler" on YouTube. Thanks & love...

C. For you to be moved (as was I) by John Wheeler's expression, you must be open, free to actually hear, Heart to Heart. I salute you for the enormous transformation that you have allowed to happen; the transcending of ego and self-centered convictions of limitation can be a threatening and unnerving process - as you well know now.

You are The One that was seeking itself. Staying with I AM and allowing nothing to distract from that Being that You are reveals the True Heart surprisingly quickly. Now you are experiencing this directly. That is great news indeed!

"Good on ya", as 'Sailor' Bob Adamson might say!

Now it's known: To stay with I AM and refuse all beliefs that follow I AM. Be as You are. You are Only Being, not the story or the storyteller. Don't sell out to false beliefs and inauthentic stories of lack and limitation. Stay in touch. I love you.

44. Stay Home!

Abide as what you ARE … No Thing. You were never born! That Absolute Being-Awareness-Aliveness IS all there is. All there is already is fully Realized. You are Nothing … appearing Nowhere … and Everywhere … as … Everything. There is NO path, NO goal, no knowledge, nothing to get and no-one to get it. Full Stop.

"I have no role to fulfill, because the 'I' is not. How can that which has no existence have a role, or any other characteristic? For this reason, I am neither awakened nor enlightened nor liberated nor any other positive statement. I am. Even the thought 'I am', I am not. Even the sense 'I am', I am not, because that sense comes and goes. I am not even conscious because consciousness comes and goes. I cannot even be said to exist, because that which is not an object cannot be or not be. I am prior to being and knowing, but the unnamable source from which they emerge. Being-awareness-peace, presence-awareness, emptiness, or any other term is only a crude pointer to what I am. I am nothing, and yet I am".

– John Wheeler

Same HERE.

45. You Are Beyond All "States"

Q: I've just been told about you, this morning. I have read Sailor Bob Adamson, Tony Parson, Ramana, Nisargadatta and very recently Jean Klein.

C. That's VERY good company you are keeping! You'll hear nothing really different here than what they are pointing you to look at and the essence of the Message is that YOU ARE what you seek. Just noticing that is a fundamental starting point in this.

Q: My stumbling block is on Enlightenment. Since we have to use words to exchange, with their limited conceptual interpretation, I will use the word "State".

C. There is NO "state of enlightenment." "States" are experiences in awareness that come and go. The classic example is of the "sage" who asked for a bowl of rice to be brought to him. Then while waiting he meditated and entered a "state of samadhi" (so-called transcendental union or oneness) … then he came out a week later, in an empty room, and looked around and shouted, where's my rice? That state passed as all states must. What is it about "you" that NEVER changes? Look at that one.

What we call enlightenment here is the simple seeing that only what never changes … your inescapable Being-Awareness-Aliveness … is Real. ALL that comes and goes is a dream-like appearance arising out of nowhere in the Absolute Being-Prior-To-Awareness … and THAT is the ONLY unchanging Reality … the so-called Eternal State. (The use of the word "state" here is poetic. It is really more accurate poetically pointed to as "The Stateless State." Words divide the whole, but only apparently!)

You are dreaming that you are awake, dreaming that you are asleep, dreaming that you are dreaming. All three "relative" states of Consciousness are dream states arising, as already said, IN or ON the Absolute Unknowing Being that you truly are (the idea of you appears in THAT … the Timeless Spaceless Unborn Absolute You…) words seem to make That an object known by a subject so do recognize that all words only point to That which is ultimately totally BEYOND describing or representation and CANNOT be grasped! In short do NOT believe or accept a word of this or any other pointer as some "truth."

Q: I understand what you and the others are saying.

C. WHO understands? Where IS this "understander?" This is NOT a matter of mentally comprehending. When a false "you" listens as "an individual" hearing another "individual" say this stuff, the message is completely missed! All you will read or hear here and from the others you mention is I AM speaking to I AM. The ONE I Am of Being Itself.

Q: But I am looking for that state where the illusion, the dream is "really" seen through. The state that Robert Adams, Bernadette Roberts, Jean Klein, Ramana etc. experienced.

C. Again: There is NO permanent "state" to be "experienced." What is being pointed to is as stated many times NOT an "experience!" That cannot be stresses too strongly. NOT an experience. YOU are NOT a concept NOR are you an "experience." You are NO THING and until that is fully understood there is no end of seeking states and blissful experiences and all that crap! It is, to be straight about it, BULLSHIT.

Q: See, I have the knowledge that you are talking about…

C. This is the mental comprehension and that is the booby prize. You must go a LOT deeper. This "knowing" or "owning knowledge" is superficial and cannot dispel suffering. WHO says "I know? Where is the "me" that asserts, "I have it?" What is it that wants a "state" that this false "I" can own? Where IS this I, this "self-centered entity" called you or me, with a name, and desires, who wants, and wants what is not already here?

Q: …but then this doesn't come with the state of these individuals, of Buddha…In Tibetan Dzogchen, they give the example of the clouds obscuring the sun. The clouds being the obscuration of the mind, the ego.

C. That is a POINTER. But this obscuration is UNREAL. We make it real then try to dispel it! That is tail chasing!

Q: They give many, numerous methods, techniques, mantras etc...etc. to enable one to reach this state. They called this state "Rigpa".

C. All that is in my view a corruption of the simplicity of this. The word Dzogchen translates as "The Great Perfection." Then that is defined as Non-Conceptual Presence-Awareness." THAT is ALL!

Notice that the ego is taken to be a "fact" where it is only an assumption of a belief in something unreal. This so-called "ego" is a fantasy, and that is NOT real to begin with! Then all manner of practices are "prescribed" to annihilate this fantasy of a false ego. But since the practices assume the fact of an ego and thereby only reinforce the illusion, how could they take the ego beyond itself? It's a totally false assumption, a faulty premise, operating unnoticed in the background of all that story of practices leading to perfection "someday!" Where IS this ego? Can you find one anywhere? Apart from a simple one-letter thought ... "I" ... which is merely a cloud-like appearance assumed in ignorance to be a thing apart from the whole, there is NO ego, and NO separation, only an IDEA of such. Can an idea, a thought, separate itself from the aliveness, awareness, in which it arises? And what is at work here that is driving the appearing thoughts of "me and the universe?" Where is a me apart from that infinite Energy that drives totality to appear as manifestation and seeming (ONLY seeming!) separate objects and separate pseudo subjects? Subject/Object ... "I/Other" ... IS the core delusion.

Q: The ego is then dissolved, what Ramana experienced as the death of the ego.

C. Actually that's a descriptive kind of "poetry." But it's absolutely NOT "the truth." How can a non-thing that never really existed in the first place die or be dissolved? It seems to appear as such in the waking dream as a seeker's sense of separation fades ... either gradually or suddenly. But when the premise or assumption driving the question or statement is wrong the answer or conclusion will also be wrong: If there is no such thing as a separate "person" how could that nonentity die?

Q: Does just "abiding in this "knowledge" lead to the "blissful" fully Realized state?

C. Abide as what you ARE … No Thing. You were never born! That Absolute Being-Awareness-Aliveness IS all there is. All there is already is fully Realized. You are Nothing … appearing Nowhere … and Everywhere … as … Everything. There is NO path, NO goal, no knowledge, nothing to get and no-one to get it. Full Stop.

46. The 'Aha' Is Always Here and Now

Q: A friend suggested visiting your videos - good stuff. Question: Was there an aha! that came upon you and under what circumstances?

C. Yes, when I met John Wheeler. John pointed out the inescapable fact of Being-Existence ... I AM. He asked, do you exist? The aha was that obviously I AM before the thought of being I Am or a being "a person" ever arises. Then he also pointed out that only a false belief in a self-center, as "me," seems (only seems! Like clouds only seem to obscure the sun!) to obscure the ever-present Being-Awareness, and that by looking into this belief and finding that it is only a false assumption, the whole paradigm of seeker-seeking-something fades and there is what is Always So ... Being-Awareness-Aliveness... just That and there is NO separation of doer in That.

The subsequent investigation seemed to take some "time" but this was actually really "done" in the instant of direct apperception. This happens only always NOW; this is a direct immediate seeing by no-one that what IS is No thing ... and That is appearing AS Every thing.

All that happens is (in a way of pointing) a clear seeing of the "story of me" IS ONLY a story and NOT the Real. All the "mind "can be used for is to uncover what is false. The Real is Unborn, Unchanging, ever fresh and not only obvious and inescapable right now but also inconceivable and unknowable. That is what IS Prior To Awareness, and allows for the arising of Awareness and the pulsating of Aliveness ... Intelligence-Energy, the Unmoved Mover of all that is. In short Nothing Appearing as everything; Pure Wisdom and Pure love.

Seeing this directly from and as Naked Being ends the search once and for good.

Q: Thanks.

Sure! :-)

47. Only A Fake Claims "I KNOW"

Q: First, thank you. It's seen now that the I is not a solid object, truly, honestly. You say I am a space, a nothing. This might be so, but so what? Nothing really changes, even though the I-thought isn't believed to be my true self, it still comes up, it doesn't die. All of "creation" is one and it looks from where I sit here that all that can be pointed to in the world, is that emptiness masquerading as form, the universe is one consciousness in a sense. But since there's no "I" to do anything - how does everything happen? Is this body just reacting to the rest and the pure emptiness is witnessing? No will anywhere? How come this miracle happen?

C. I am happy to hear from you. Now let's be clear...

1. Don't believe what I say!! Looking for yourself is what this is about, NOT believing any pointer or any so-called "other."

2. NOTHING happens. All this is about is seeing the false as false and the real as real. Nothing will happen! That's the spiritual bullshit ... "waiting for some big enlightenment thing to happen." You wrote, *It's seen now that the I is not a solid object, truly, honestly.* STOP HERE!

3. You still want to know how and why! Asked and answered already. Re-read the previous e-mails.

Q: ....and don't think I don't know what you're going to say: "Who's asking the questions? Find the source of this "I". There's nothing there." Yes I get it. But nothing really changes, it won't disappear forever.

C. The mind is way too arrogant, claiming "I KNOW" what YOU are going to say! Just notice that ... here is what actually is here to say:

The "I" as a thought of sense of being a person need not disappear and most likely will NOT until the physical body dies! All that is being pointed to is a false IDENTIFICATION with the "I" thought. Seeing the false AS false is what this is all about. Then suffering abates and is finally gone forever as there is no sense that life is happening "to me." There is Life Itself and you are that, including ALL thoughts. Waiting for the "I" to "disappear" will have that "I" around still "believed in" and looking for its own absence (!) and that can bring suffering. One who waits, waits forever. See right now that YOU ARE and THAT is KNOWN beyond doubt. Everything else is a story and just let the story be without attaching yourself as a person telling a story ... being a story and a storyteller. Let it BE. No resistance no problems! As to saying "I got it," that's just another thought story. Drop it and BE.

You are sitting here: 'you are'. Prior to words. Now the hearsay goes 'I am', 'I am' means the flow of the mind has started. Now whatever you say with that 'I am-ness' through the mind about 'you', you have represented as yourself. But that is not so.

– Sri Nisargadatta Maharaj (courtesy of Pradeep Apte, aptep@yahoo.com.)

48. What Thinks, And Judges Itself?

J.O. Writes, I'm beginning to think that either I'm not smart enough to understand this or too afraid to put out the effort required to understand. What little understanding I have of the basics, that I am Awareness, does not seem to go any deeper than, I am Aware of the world right now. There are moments, very brief moments, of some insight, but no understanding as to how that could be what or where my freedom is. Maybe my understanding of what it means to be free, awake, enlightened, etc. is still that flash of illuminating wisdom that takes away all problems, fears, confusion and leaves one in state of ceaseless rapture, (which I know is false). Whatever it is or isn't I cannot find it here.

C. WHO thinks these things? Have you noticed that thoughts just "show up" unbidden? If it is you thinking, why do "you" think these negative thoughts about yourself? And what is the point of these self-damning sentences? Why would you want to limit your true Self? What is thinking? What is moving the thoughts to arise? They are not there in deep sleep. In sleep there is no you and the body lives just fine without your control or thought. So, WHO is the thinker here? You? If so, stop thinking and be. If not, have a look.

As we repeat often, stay with the basics as best you can: You know you ARE. That is all there is to get, that Being IS and you are that. Inescapable and yet the mind cannot grasp that. If that is not accepted, who disagrees? Who do you take yourself to be? A thing apart from All That Is? Who does that? You are what you seek. Full Stop.

Q: I enjoy your site and am hoping to take part in the call-in service that you have.

C. You are always welcome. Stay in touch.

49. I Am, Therefore I Love

Remember……..

Nothing in this book is real.

Nothing in this book is true.

This book points to something you do not know that you do not know. That is not a thing that words can describe, evoke, or represent.

Without one or more of those, what is left?

Nothing.

Also "known" by "no-one" as

Paradise.

The Home You Never Left.

Q: How do I tell the truth from the false?

C. That's easy. It's ALL false. Like my buddy Werner sometimes said, "All there IS is Bullshit, and Nothin'..."!

And my dear friend John Greven, author of "Oneness," notes: "Here's a 'Litmus Test' - If ANYTHING is assumed to be other than bullshit – then there is something wrong with the perspective".

So even "bullshit AND nothin'" is a false perspective!

There IS no "true perspective".

Full Stop.

THIS is LOVE. The Love that surpasses "understanding".

Part Two: Was Paradise Ever Lost?

This book is named "Paradise Found".

(But wait – was Paradise Ever Lost??)

Paradise Lost?

Before Finding Paradise, it seems that paradise is lost
and must be sought after....

Much Ado About Nothing

50. There Is Nothing To "Stabilize" As

Q: I have been what one might call a serious "seeker" for approximately the last thirty-five years. After much "exploration" I gravitated toward non-duality / Advaita Vedanta and have studied most of the biggies within this area, both old and new. This "realization" has been much more than intellectual / conceptual but stabilization has not taken place. I am attaching a short description below that I wrote not long after one "moment" of clarity followed by months of what I might call "enlightened living" to give you a flavor of what was "experienced"... yet stabilization has not occurred.

C. There is no such thing as "stabilization". This notion is a product of the belief in a myth, the myth of stasis or endless experiential bliss or peace. Perfect Peace IS what you are and all experiences arise from, last a while if they do, and disappear back into that fathomless emptiness that You actually are. There is NO hanging on to Awareness ... it's NO Thing! How can Nothing hang on to Itself? It is NOT "much MORE than" ... it is MUCH LESS than!

Q: I have one tiny question that has been pricking at me. I would be very interested to know your "opinion", if you have one.

C. Let me respond regarding "my opinion," with a quote from The Hsin Hsin Ming: "If you wish to know the truth, then hold to no opinions for or against anything." And, "Do not seek for the truth; only cease to cherish opinions. Do not remain in a dualistic state; avoid such easy habits carefully." These point to the brute fact that Being, Awareness, Aliveness Itself, are BEYOND opinions and such concepts serve only to reinforce the erroneous belief that there is a believer and an opiner." There is NOT and investigation proves that beyond any doubt. The classic pointer is to inquire, to ASK the mind-opinion-maker, What ARE YOU? Directly, asking "Who Am I" or "What Am I" is a working investigation into the false; when the false is revealed as false only the Real can remain. And what IS the Real? That Space of Being-Prior-To-Consciousness that NEVER changes.

Q: Specifically, if one "believes" that who/ what they truly are in essence is Pure Awareness/ Presence Awareness/ Unlimited Consciousness/ etc. then eventually the "me" or the "I" will be seen for what it is (not) and though it may not completely "go away" it will certainly take a back seat. Now this "recognition/ realization" of who/ what I AM generally begins as a mental construct/ concept and opens into a deep apperception (non-mental). My question is, "Might not any 'liberating' mental construct ultimately produce the same or similar result?" "As you believe in your heart, so you are."

C. In a word, NO. There are NO "liberating concepts." Concepts are dry inherently empty meaningless words, and while words can POINT, they CANNOT "liberate." A good question for you might be, "What IS the Source of 'apperception'?" No answer, ONLY the inquiry! The Inquest (investigation of the facts of a situation).

It needs to be understood that this seeing-knowing is NOT a matter of belief. What is pointed to is that the Reality that you are is BEYOND beliefs and believer, known and knower. This what the term "apperception" points to … in This there is NO perceiver! No believer! All the believer can do is agree or disagree, and the empty Awareness that You are simply sees and registers all the appearing pairs of opposites … THIS is BEYOND description, BEYOND belief or disbelief, BEYOND all concepts and all experiences.

The only thing the mind can say to what the True nature of This is, is Not That Not This Not That Not This. In the remaining Not-Knowing what IS, is the bliss of true Freedom. THIS IS LITERALLY NO Thing! The thought-story called "believer-me" can NEVER grasp This. It is simply OPEN, EMPTY, OBVIOUS, and can neither be attained nor lost.

Q: Here are a few of the "concepts" to which I am alluding… This is all a dream, therefore none of it is real and "I" and "other" are not and are therefore not good, bad, innocent, guilty, right, wrong, etc.

C. Yes, when it is seen that "you" are a dream-character, a phantom taken as real only in ignoring the Emptiness of The Real.

Q: There is no "doer", therefore I and other never did anything and are therefore blameless and pure.

C. Yes and NOT as a "belief."

Q: Really "we" are just thoughts, and as such non-existent, and therefore perfect no-thing.

C. Seeing this is a step. Now drop THIS knowing, drop ALL knowing. Knowing No Thing, is Being Everything.

Q: I was born under a "special" star and am therefore blessed and perfect with infinite awareness.

C. You were NEVER born.

Q: My Father and I are One; therefore "I" am free/ freedom. No-thing is, therefore, since "I" seem to be experiencing, it is True that I AM That I AM. AM perfect awareness now and as such I am perfectly aware now. My "teacher" tells me that "I AM That" and he's a pretty smart fellow, so he must be right and I must be That. My concept is that I am everything/ nothing, therefore I will awaken to that "reality" ETC, etc., etc.

C. See the utter falseness in this statement? I am that I am, I am awareness ... (BUT!) when will "I" awaken? You will never "awaken to this." You are already This and seeking that reinforces the tail-chasing seeker. It's utter ignorance (ignoring the Real and adopting a stance of being a separate "I-person" entity that wants to get somewhere someday.) It's all a pattern of ignorant mind-belief. This is delusion and suffering. The cure is investigation ... starting from the FACT that YOU ARE THIS I AM and that is inescapable; then looking for a separate controller called "me" that wants to attain emptiness ...! Where IS that I? It's not "your" father. I and That (called "father" by an insecure ego seeking a "big daddy") ARE One. That One is known in mind as I AM THAT I AM and nothing else. IT AIN'T Personal! Freedom IS but not for a "you" or an "I." You cannot attain Freedom; You ARE Freedom (Liberation).

Look: WHO is thinking-believing-typing-knowing all that? What ARE You in Reality? NO concept or experience can describe That. You are Unborn, Being arising as Awareness expressing as impersonal absolute Aliveness.

Q: The point is that there are thousands upon thousands of mental "concepts" (perhaps all "true" or all "false") that can help bring about favorable conditions in one's psychology to assist in an awaking, but they are all only and just concepts/ thoughts. And perhaps we simply shape our experience of "reality" based on our points of view. As consciousness, we shape our dream, which is only consciousness.

C. Lovely words, but NO concept is either true or false. NONE. Period. Full Stop! The "point of view" is the ignorance of mind that conceives itself as separate from the whole. Investigate this! There IS NO separate "we!" All Is The One. Witnessing, Seeing, Being-As-Consciousness. EMPTY.

Q: The essence of this question may be lost in the words, so please excuse any muddled expression. I'm confident that if "clarity" were consciously present (with "me") the question simply might not arise, but since that is not the current "state" consciously, the question surfaces.

C. Who is asking the questions? What makes the mind think, the fingers type, the brain erupt in thoughts of "me myself and I? What makes you wake up as Consciousness? Where's this "me" that thinks it is real and lacks some clarity!? There is The One, NO Thing, and then out of One No Thing No Where comes a Being-Awareness "I AM." ASK YOU: What is the source of that I AM?

Stay with the only thing that IS and beyond doubt? YOU ARE. This IS of Being-Awareness arises as a direct, real, authentic and inexhaustible I AM and this is absolute freedom. All else is bondage and unreal. Stay with the REAL of Being, Just That.

Q: Many thanks... and I'm hoping to be back to you for an hour-long consultation soon.

C. That'll be fun! It's really "all done with mirrors!"

51. Awareness Is Not Two

Question from a YouTuber - The way you look into the audience reminds me of Ramana Maharshi. I have a simple question for you and I will be brief. The thing is this. There are 2 types of awareness. The direct one, which is thoughts, feelings, vibrations in your body. You are aware of them directly. It seems that there is no choice. In this I understand that I am the awareness.

C. There are not "two types of Awareness" in Reality. There IS Awareness and THAT is Not Two (This is the pointer – the essence – of Nonduality - or "Advaita.") All that describable stuff is NOT Awareness; that's the content of Awareness. Choiceless Content-less Awareness IS and this is what You are in Ultimate Reality. THAT never changes. All changing manifesting experiencing arises, as a product of the core human beliefs in time and location and a separate person we call I, then hangs out a little or a long while, and disappears back into That. While Awareness Plus Content are Not Two they appear as two or many.

Only in thoughts – words – is there the idea of parts of the Whole. It's ALL The Whole. As a friend, Chuck Hillig, puts it, The (W)hole in One.

Q: There is a second kind of awareness, which is the indirect type such as being aware of the movement of your hands, blinking of the eyes and breathing.

C. Some call that the witnessing Consciousness, the natural state of I AM. This I AM of Consciousness is an arising out of I – Awareness or Beingness itself. And this witnessing Consciousness is a content arising is Awareness.

Q: There are moments in which I am not aware of my breath but still someone is doing the breathing.

C. Is there someone doing? Or is that an assumption, a belief? Test this assertion that the mind makes, the claim of doing by a doer. FIND that doer, that someone. Can you? Looking for this is the investigation of the mental assumptions that cause suffering. The core is, "there is someone" and then that attaches to "me' and I am breathing is the false claim. Breathing is happening with NO doer or cause! Ponder that rather than taking it as a belief, though! Look where pointing is pointing, don't try to figure it out. The Ultimate Being is BEYOND the mind's thoughts, feelings, experiences and assumptions. ONLY in NOT Knowing is there True Seeing. Drop all knowing and BE.

Q: So I try to rephrase my conclusion saying ' I am aware that this person is breathing'. How can I overcome these doubts I keep having with the indirect type of awareness?

C. All conclusions are mental and ultimately false. All knowledge is actually ignorance posturing as knowledge. Ignorance is to leave the sanctity of Not Knowing for the paltry gifts of the mind's attachments to gaining knowledge to add to a false person. That is the false persona; the mask over Being that seems to hide your Tue Nature of Emptiness Being Fullness.

Now, what are doubts? Thoughts arising in this Timeless Spaceless Awareness that manifests as I AM. Stay at I AM and refuse all appendages to that simplicity. Look for the I that wants to overcome, that personal entity that sees what is as a problem. Challenge these mental gyrations of false beliefs and assumptions. Stay with what you know BEYOND all doubt: YOU ARE. That is all there is to see and be. Being-Awake-Alive as all that is and is not. Right here, right now, YOU ARE. Be that and add nothing to that. You are already free; just challenge the lies of the head and dwell as Timeless Being. Simple, as you were never NOT That. Love!

52. Still No Sense Of Oneness

Q: It's been a few days since this awareness of what IS happened. It is always present, but easily gives way to day-to-day thoughts and the "work-stuff" I seem to be doing. Things seem to happen as before, but this clear space that is always here remains unchanged by them. Unpleasant feelings are still felt, but noticed only as feelings. Although a lot more is being noticed there is no sense of "oneness". Even though there is noticing that everything appears in this Awareness there is still a sense of "separation". When the question "who am I" is asked, that too is seen to be "floating" in awareness. The old feeling of "who cares" which I thought went with non-attachment is replaced with "it's all OK".

C. Both a sense of Oneness and the absence of a sense of Oneness ARE Oneness! This is "Unity" and Unity includes all diversity. But it sounds like you are still striving to be an "enlightened person." That will simply never happen; what we are pointing to is self-TRANSCENDENCE. Transcendental consciousness is That stateless state in and on which the relative states of waking, dreaming, and deep sleep, arise. This so called "fourth state" is NOT an experience or a concept, as we say all the time here. It is not actually a "state" at all. It is What Is.

This cannot be described or held onto; it is absolutely beyond mind and feeling. Self-knowledge consists in Unknowing, Transcending all. Nothing special! Obvious and empty.

This Transcendent Awareness is NOT an attainment and at the same time is never absent. Don't try to figure this out! "The answer is NOT in the mind." This, Transcendence, is UN-figure-out-able.

Bottom line? What IS, Is Unicity. Both "The Relative" AND "The Absolute" are appearing IN the One AND AS the One.

All Is One.

NOT Two .....

LOVE!

Q: There does not seem to be much of a "me" left. Pain is felt as pain in the body, but not so much as "my pain". Thoughts and all else seem to occur in THIS. But you are right about this: the mind is still active and there are the old expectations of what "an Enlightened person should feel like" (oxymoron). There doesn't seem to be anyone to care about it, though. The me-ing fades and the Be-ing is clearer.

C. Yet both are happenings in/of Transcendent Awareness.

53. Out Here

Out Here in This Field
I Am You
You Are I

Out Here In The Now
Beyond All Dreams Of Being
Here, We Are

In Love

With

Love

54. Appearances Change, You Do Not

Q: Over the last few days I have oscillated between a sort of mentally-blank awareness of what is and intense thought activity. I have also noticed a marked increase in mental suffering... I have been unusually discontented and even a bit angry. Nothing external changed in my life to bring about this change... I think it might be my ego 'fighting back' or something. Do you have any ideas on how to deal with this?

C. Let it be. The false identity can seem to die hard. You are quite right that this is a seeming ego struggle to avoid the being found to be only a dream. Like the dream, happy or nightmarish, at night, waking out of happens and the dreamer has no control over when. Having been through some things like you describe I tell you with confidence, it does pass!

Also notice that everything that happens ... everything! ... arises IN the clear awareness. This, Awareness, is NOT an experience that comes and goes. Put the focus on what never changes and reject all the changing movements of thought and emotion (it's not forceful; just refuse to give any energy of belief to these moving changing appearances; they are like changing weather appearing in the empty sky. Your true nature of Being, obvious and undeniable, is what never changes. Give yourself over to That. Notice the desire to control things. Let that go - let that be.) Love ya.

55. Who Cares??

Q: If, say, all humans dies in a nuclear war in a few seconds, meaning, the Noosphere would cease to be -- would Emptiness, The capital s Self, The Dao, The Absolute, God, Spirit, Brahman, Is-ness, Such-ness, Thus-ness, This-ness, I Am, etc etc, or simply: Consciousness, still exist? I am of course referring to what these words are "pointing to", not any concepts.

C. The words are pointing to NOTHING.

Q: If no: Ok, business as usual. If yes: Ok, what makes you believe that? Is that belief somewhat more real or true than the belief of a religious, dogmatic person, and if yes, why?

C. The mind, which endlessly seeks answers to secure itself, (impossible though that is!), will HATE this reply. (Unless it doesn't.) It may poke something though. We'll have to see if that happens.

The answer is Yes-No. Or if you prefer, No-Yes. But that is only the interim relative answer. The TRUE answer (True? Speaking oxymoronically now) is …It is neither yes nor no. THIS is absolutely BEYOND beliefs AND any "believer." The pointer of Nonduality is that the idea of a "believing me" is false and if that is operating the investigation is called for. What IS a believer? Who believes anything and accepts some and rejects others? That is all the ignorance of a mind that believes its own lies, the basic lie being I am ME and I believe this or that and I don't believe this or that. It is all, to be a bit blunt, pure bullshit.

Q: Do you have any evidence to support the claim of a Consciousness that doesn't just arise because of the brain, but that the brain in fact itself arises independently within that very Consciousness?

C. I ask you this: WHO CARES? Are you suffering? If so we can address that. But speculating and asserting and trying to prove one concept to be true and another to be false sticks you into the head and there ain't NO freedom in that dark place. So I decline to engage in that. I am sure you will find plenty of people who will enjoy arguing opinions and concepts. I am not one of 'em. Respectfully I suggest you look at WHO wants to know and what will that knowing do to end suffering? This is really about a huge gift ... the gift of Unknowing. Freedom consists BEYOND knowledge, which is essentially just memory and imagination.

Q: If you say: "Well, what is that is aware of the question you just asked?" I could say, it is my consciousness which exists only because of my brain and it is only I as a separate individual (brain) who can be aware of the thoughts which arise within my mind. And you can say: "And what is aware of THAT?" And I will continue to be boring and say that it is still my awareness which is "produced" by my own brain, and if the brain dies, along with it goes the awareness or consciousness, so then I wouldn't be aware of anything any longer, because I would be dead.

C. You are already dead. LIFE consists in NOT KNOWING and simply BEING what you are, which is Unchanging Being-Awaring-Living Freedom. If you seek proof for that you will have to seek it within yourself; no one can give you what you are. There is NO evidence for what you are ... evidence is in the domain of true-false and that IS the mind-stuff that ignores that it is empty and meaningless. And by the way it is pure ignorant arrogance for anyone to claim that they are enlightened or "know the truth and can prove it" and can thereby give you that final answer (another oxymoron) about the No Thing which YOU already are in Reality.

Q: Short: Does consciousness exist outside a person's brain? And isn't that a belief? And if no, why?

C. Yes, No, and LOOK for yourself. Find out if there really IS a believer, an I that knows. When you do this you find what you are ... NOTHING. Empty and Meaningless. And THAT don't mean a damn thing either! Nonduality is NOT for believers! There are churches, mosques, synagogues, monasteries and ashrams for that. There is NO food for your ego here. There is however, absolute unconditional Love.

56. There Are No "Accurate Pointers"

Q: Is it an accurate pointer to say that there are no thoughts, emotions, and experiences? Rather there is think-ING, feel-ING, and experience-ING all happening within the limitless spaciousness of be-ING??

C. If that pointer resonates, it resonates. BUT there are NO "accurate pointers." They're all words and meaningless ultimately...

If a pointer resonates FOR YOU it might be judged, "I rather like that one". It's somewhat similar to the way Bob Adamson points to this pointless space-ING Being... in this way it might seem to one organism to be "more accurate" than a different pointer that does not. Yet that other one that doesn't strike a chord for you, in your heart so to say, may well resonate in another bodymind and quicken some direct apperception of what is pointed to.

So ultimately it's paradoxically (again with the paradoxically!) an "individual matter" as in the appearance all are unique. No two organisms resonate in exactly the same way; all are unique expressions of The One Energy-Being, as are no two snowflakes alike yet all are made of water.

If it lights YOUR fire it's good. If not toss it out like the useless bathwater but keep the baby, the Essence, Essence-ING.

Love ya!

57. Being Is One-Oneness-ING

Follows-up: Another important pointer (I "think")...came to me...WHAT IS, IS.

C. What IS IS? Nah. There IS NO IS. Zero Stasis. No Stop. Only Stop-ING. Everything ING-ING. Stillness-ING :-)

What appears IS. ... IS-ING. Life-ING. Aliveness-ING.

Code Word: BE-ING.

Only That No Thing No-Thing-ING!

WERDZ! Werd-ING Funny-ING ??!!

HA!

Love-ING, Charlie-ING

Q: ! "I laughed, I cried, I felt everything!" Beautiful! IS=subjective. If it "is" happening, it's happening to someone.

IS-NESS=objective...a part of the fullness of Being and inseparable from the One.

THIS E-MAIL=more tail-chasing? HA

I love you, Charlie...and I can feel the love from your responses!

C. Bang! And the Love is You

Only Love, Allways

Youing-ING/Charlieing-ING

58. Is-Ing, Life-ING, Big Bang Bang-ING

Follow-up: Thanks for your response...your feedback from the vantage point of stillness is very helpful. From time to time, these pointers pop into my head. With your permission, I'd like to continue sharing them with you and have you tell "me" from the space of awareness whether or not they point toward or away from truth.

C. Of course. But there is NO "vantage point of stillness. This Is-ness is pointless. Stillness both IS and IS NOT and unknowably ungraspably indescribably REAL. Ha! Werdz ...

Q: Last night I was thinking (oops!) about the pointer I AM and my experience in the world. Another important pointer (I "think")...came to me...WHAT IS, IS. All my life, to this point, has been an effort to "figure it all out." I've wanted to know the Answer. Thus the futility of my 15 year spiritual seeking. Lately, it's become apparent to me that my knowing is not only unnecessary, but is actually keeping me on the hamster wheel.

C. Exactly. Yet, who does this? No-one. Who thinks I? Who owns "my life?" No-one. It happens as a functioning of The Cosmic Game we call Life (Life, Life-ING.) No owner no doer only Living ING-ing.

Q: There's a great line from A Course In Miracles that came to me (I paraphrase): "Surrender your delusion that your understanding can make a significant (any) contribution to the truth." "I" don't need to know (as if that were actually possible) where my thoughts, emotions and experiences come from. "My" task is to stay centered in the I AM and let WHAT IS, IS (awkward, but you get my point). Thoughts, emotions, and experiences arise in the "I don't know," Linger for awhile, and return to the space of "I don't know."

C. Yes, and words are only appearing to be solid, appearing as a tool of mind apparently dividing (only apparently); can a word ACTUALLY divide the Whole? No but it seems so, until it's seen that words are bubbles of being arising from nowhere.) As you say: these bubbles of nothing arise as the seeming-something in the "I don't know."

Q: I can watch it all go by like a 4th of July parade.

C. YOU as the Appearance of Witnessing Consciousness (I AM) which bubbles into beingness out of Just I (I-No-Thing and not even That!) ...THAT I AM watches with zero attachment and zero involvement. Empty loving presence ... presence-ING.

Suffering arises when "you" think that there is a you that authored all of this...grabbing one of those thoughts out of the sky and declaring that it describes something about me. Once that's done, the mind goes about analyzing and categorizing the thought...what does it mean to ME?...is it good or bad for ME? As long as "I" refrain from attaching any "personal" significance to what I'll call Life, my "self-making" days are over and I am free...nothing to know or understand...

That IS what happens to be happen-ing and notice that you didn't author THAT either ... there is nothing to do when there is no-one and all do-ing happens as the happen-ING of Life Life-ING. There WAS no "Big Bang." No creation. No creator. Nothing ever happened AND there is THIS, This-ING, Happen-ING. The Big Bang-ING. WERDZ! What great FUN!

Q: I guess the message is, "you have no control, so just sit back and enjoy the ride."

C. No. The message is LOOK and see if there IS any controller in you or anyone or anywhere controlling!? Sit back, enjoy the ride? Sounds good. Why wouldn't everyone - especially seeker-everyones - DO that? What is in charge of that happening or not? Who is gonna CONTROL that? LOL ... Ride-ING happen-ING but only appear-ING. Apperceive-ING This is the Final No-stepper-Step-ING off the Cliff into No Where and No Thing WOW Everything ING.

Q: Is this the peace of "not knowing?"

C. Is IT? Is there any IS? This Is It, IT-ING. Nothing special! (That's not special either!)

Love!

140

59. Nothing Special; Simply Being

Q: At some point listening to you on the conference call, there was an undercutting of the I, following which words seemed to register on the forehead but not enter the brain and then emerge as concepts (to choose some descriptive words).

C. Excellent seeing. Give the concepts no entry and nothing can stick to the empty fullness that You are. As The One removes the false props on which the ego stands, the person drops into Nowhere and there is only No-person, Everywhere. (to spout some more descriptive words for what IS and yet IS Indescribable!)

Q: Later I went to a satsang. The leader was explaining to someone that unhappiness comes, goes, comes; happiness comes, goes, comes. There was an awareness that unhappiness or happiness implies a me who is unhappy or happy, and this "me" is a fiction; it does not exist. I started to softly chuckle. As also noted on the call, along with the undercutting of the I, and the words not rebounding in the skull, there was a gratifying sense of resolution of paradox, e.g., form being emptiness. Wanted to report and say thanks.

C. That sounds great. This is the natural state ... Being-Awake-Alive, living from the eternal utterly ordinary peace of being nothing special and just this. That was never missing, only overlooked. Correct the core mistake of identity, the conviction "I am the body," and the life sentence in the prison of the mind is overturned. Let's call that Amnesty! Freedom. Or "early release" ... as the Zen Master Bankei put it, this is to "die before you die."

Now stay with that natural Unborn I-before the I and refuse to accept the false assertion of a phantom! Much love to you, E.J. Thank you for sharing this. I Love You.

What does not change is real.

What changes is only appearance.

- John Greven

60. "Teachings" Are A Distraction

You can listen to CDs of "teachings" endlessly. Doing that will never end the search ... rather that "doing" more often than not just reinforces the false notion that you are NOT already whole and complete, that you are a separate being apart from your own wholeness, and that something is wrong that you are endlessly trying and failing to fix! You simply cannot EVER fill that empty longing for home with temporal concepts or experiences, all of which come and go! You'll never get enough of what is false to make the true appear! Instead of that why not rest quietly in what IS ... awareness, present and alive, unchanging and serene?

Then regarding a desire for listening to such CDs (anyone's including mine for that matter! LOL...) ask your mind- the "I-other" storyteller that plagues you - Who is listening? Why? To become convinced that what you are is Timeless Being? That's a denial OF That which you are; you give way to the mind's addiction to "I am ME!" and thereby continue to suffer. I am speaking sharing direct experience here, NOT theory or "teachings" like most CDs and books, and NOT from spiritual concepts or jargon!

These CDs seem to give a rush of experience that feels good but when they stop that feeling goes and whatever your assumed default state is resumes. It's like having a few martinis which feels great while it's happening but the hangover really sucks, right? This is the same thing! The seeker is an addict in search of a fix. What we ignore in listening to these endless CDs and whatnot is that we already ARE that which is sought and the seeking of that DENIES us That. So the seeking IS suffering....

The understanding these various talkers describe may be seem "accurate" but that is ONLY a description and the description is NOT the Real No Thing that YOU are!

Just recognize here and now that these elegant-seeming expressed understandings are not the "end of all ends". Intellectual grasping is the booby prize! It is nothing but mistaking the feeling-thought story of "me" and "my life" as a "spiritual person" for the actual Endless Being of unconditioned unbounded Love that you really are. Stop seeking and here you are, whole and complete, awareness without beginning or end. Start seeking again and that seems to be masked or covered over but IS awareness actually masked? AWARENESS IS. You are That. Can you move out of or away from awareness? Never. No. Not possible!

Here is the final point: If ANYTHING - including these pointers for "understanding" - is assumed to be other than ignorance – then that creates a perspective that is absolutely only more ignorance. There is NO "truth". All "teachings" are bullshit.

What happens here is NOT a "teaching" and not "understanding". If a label is wanted then it is best called a "sharing" - Of The One with The One. I AM to I AM. In Timeless Love.

Do get this last pointless point, said another rather more direct way by my friend John Greven, author of "Oneness": If ANYTHING is assumed to be other than bullshit – then there is something wrong with the perspective.

"Who am I" can be the final solvent that erases the false. leaving what You already ARE ... wholeness, One-Essence, Energy-Being-Aliveness ... just That and no thing else. Refuse all except THAT. Listening to talkers droning on about this is a distraction and not really helpful in the end!

THAT is THAT!

61. Just BE

Follow-up: I don't have to do anything. In fact, there's absolutely nothing I can do. Welcome every nasty, brutish, or wondrous and beatific thought or feeling equally as an expression of the Divine Intelligence.

Love, hate, jealousy, passion are all threads in the grand tapestry of Consciousness.

All I have to do...right this moment...is to BE. Such joy. Such liberation. Freedom at last. Love, J.

C. Bang ON!

Very well done.

Game Over. Love ya!

Does awareness have a place where it starts? Does it have a place where it ends? Does it appear to be bound by time? Is it now or ever changing? Did it get older as the body aged? Is it constant or moving? Do you expect that it will ever be different? Can you, even for a moment, get out of it? If thinking stopped would you still be aware? Does anything affect that awareness? Is it your awareness or is it just awareness? It is the real and on that the world of change and illusion appears.

–*John Greven*

62. This Is Oneness. There Is ONLY Oneness.

What NEVER changes? Oneness Itself. Nothing-Everything. An IDEA of being a "separate person" can come and go ... so what? All perspectives are false. No perspective is real. ONLY No-Perspective is Real. :-) Oneness is what you ARE and That is NOT a concept NOR an experience. NOT a "perspective". All of that comes and goes on the screen of Awareness Itself ... appearing and dissolving ... In and AS The One That IS... This Timeless Love that is simply beyond description.

M.S. says, Beautiful work Charlie! Your continual pointing and shining the pen light into the eyes for awakening is incredible, and - very inspiring to me. I look at the struggle here and see the one grasping to find itself, the search and struggle is wonderful. If there were no desire there would not be that conversation at all. "Words are our longing for home" - *Rumi* - keep it up with the whacking stick you swing it well!!!:). Your friend ... M.

C. I am, as always, out of control here. It all happens! I watch in wonder! Love, you, M!

If you attach even to a trace

of this and that, of right and wrong,

the Mind-essence will be lost in confusion.

Although all dualities arise from the One,

do not be attached even to ideas of this One.

- Seng T'San, The Hsin Hsin Ming

63. There Is No 'God' And You Are 'God'

What IS The "I" Really?

The I is an imaginary character you have assumed is the real you only in innocence. It's like you believe in Santa Claus. The tooth fairy. The "I" - me. You must give up all childish beliefs. These "entities" including the so-called "me-entity", the core misunderstanding which arrived at around age two, are ALL fictional. That primordial illusion that all the rest depend on, this "I" idea, was the first to come and is nearly always the last to go. The fictional "me", is always the last illusion to be disillusioned of!

That "I" simply needs to be seen and understood for what it is ... nothing but a thought with no substantiality ... just bubbling energy arising in Timeless Awareness. Yet YOU ARE so that "I" MUST represent something. It does! The sound "I" POINTS to awareness, which is always so and prior to time and thought. That is always here now wherever you are and whatever you think. Stop searching and there (Here) You are, simple awareness, free and clear. This is The Eternal Is and all your problems are completely imaginary. All is taken care of. You need not meddle with Nature. She brings the organism everything it needs when it needs it. It could NOT be otherwise. Trust THAT.

YOU ARE AWARENESS, NOT the "thought-story", the imaginary waking-dream character which appears and disappears in thought. All the time you take your actual being to be this thought you try to get that thought back to wholeness, which just reinforces the sense of being a thing apart from other things and from "God" or The One.

There are NOT "two I Am's" - I AM is universal, singular. That is The Timeless One which YOU know as your sense of being ... your very Is-ness ... the knowing YES I AM ... but that sense of Being is neither thought nor feeling. It is simply awareness. Just that! It's this serene, blank, accepting, empty space of knowing, I AM which encompasses all that appears within it in unconditioned, Infinite, Impersonal Love. You are Love. Nothing more, nothing less!

Naturally you do know that YOU ARE. That is NO Thing. Know yourself this way: "That, I Am". "I Am That". This is the ancient pointer to what You are, NOW, Here, Eternally. Just This and NO other! This is "Advaita" – "Not Two." NON duality.

Without taking a thought, and considering a thought to be what you are, where is any is separate "you" that is not surrendered to a separate "God?" Who would surrender to whom?? A thought? Can a thought do ANYTHING? It's just a thought that comes and goes in awareness. You are that awareness, NOT that thought. This I-apart from other - and God - is a story of suffering. Look for the one telling the story. Do you find any separate thing apart from thoughts about thoughts? A vicious circle of falsehoods? To say it as directly as can be noted in language: There IS No God and YOU Are God. Sit with that, like you're letting a pillow rest in your lap.

64. A Feeling Of Lacking Something

Q: Sometimes there is certain feeling of lacking something. I didn't tell you about it before because it's not always there, it comes and goes. This is an appearance in "I Am" but certainly is a bit bothering. There is no problem but I feel a "tendency or desire" for this to stop.

C. The "feeling of lacking" IS the false center (usually called 'ego') wanting more or different than what is at this moment. This moment and not even that is Real. Being IS. Unknowable. If there is feeling lack, who feels it? Who is bothered? Botherations happen! So what? Who does that? No-one. Who can stop that? No-one. It happens until it doesn't ... "this too shall pass." So all this appears and happens in Timeless Being, Unborn and eternally free. And you know that YOU are THAT, beyond the beyond, nowhere and everywhere and beyond even that ... freedom!

There is no past except in thought; there is no future except in thought. There is no present except in thought, there is only right now and it is so immediate that the mind can't grasp it.

- John Greven

65. YOU Are Transparent & Inescapable

Follow-up: I just finished listening to your consultation with J.H. a few days ago and one part struck me very much that when he 'didn't get it' that there is no knowing of 'it' but just - being-.....transcended. That's a crucial point, there is no knowing or owning - that's part of the story, yet - I, "the smart one" likes to fall into this trap........

C. You are seeing that clearly ... and yet ... the story about that is NOT that as you are noticing here. And at the same time, that very story arises in this Transparent Being-Awakeness that You are in Reality... by the way there is some follow-up from J.H. that you may have seen on the website correspondence page; he actually did see it... as the One-Essence boiled away some of the false.

Q: You mentioned that you had once had suicidal thoughts and I had them too between the age of about 16 and my early thirties (I am 48) - they were actually quite comforting during these times of suffering (as a way out of suffering).... I still have depressions (mild ones) occasionally but I see them simply as passing clouds and they are quickly gone.

C. Yep. That was always the case! It was just an ignoring of the Space of your Being that had us ever take such thoughts to be "me" and/or "about me." Suffering? Then suicidal thoughts? Stormy weather! Comfort? Eye of the storm! Nothing special, just weather. Appearing in the empty unborn space of Awareness.

Q: I wonder sometimes how you distinguish between experiences and 'it'?

C. You can see the distinctness in your direct experience, first thing on waking in the morning, there is immediate Awareness; then the thought I arises as I, I Am, I am me, I must get up, make coffee etc. This is the Absolute Being-Awareness arising out of Nowhere into Being-Awakeness and that is the relative appearing IN the Absolute. Then identification as an entity happens, the overlay of a me on what is. "Disturbing the peace," apparently (but ONLY apparently). So as far as that goes there is a distinction ... Being is Emptiness and arises as Awakeness. Check it out after the next session of deep sleep. Now: WHO "distinguishes? To distinguish there much be a distinction-maker, and the suggestion is to LOOK for that controller of thought, that "maker of distinction", and see if you can locate such an entity anywhere.

Q: In 1984, I was sitting in a car on the passenger seat, it was quiet and then sunrise came and I was watching the outside landscape when I suddenly felt in peace with no thoughts for I don't know how long but it was very powerful and subtle at the same time (it had a strong impact on me and might be the cause for my search). Looking back now (the knowledge of memory - LOL) I must have just 'been' - something what I subtly would like to have and probably unconsciously believe that is it what to look for.

C. That happened IN what you are and was NOT the "goal." It was, simply, a happening, like the weather is a happening. So that was like a warm sunny day where other days are stormy and thunderous. And you are quite right to question if that fleeting experience is the actual Natural, Eternal Statelessness that the seeker seeks, OR simply another weather pattern that comes and goes IN The Eternal State that we are.

Q: I know, I know, it's a trap - looking for a result in the future what is there right here right now.... Hard to let go though since this is something I like to cling to (subtly), so you must play hardball with me too - permission granted :-)

C. You say I know. WHO knows? There is only knowing; the knower is an illusion, a story of an ignorant mind-entity that is unreal and yet asserts its reality and is believed by the idiot mind itself. All self-referential! A tautology.

And ... If you are "trying to let go" of some attachment to a preference, fond memory, unwanted thoughts or emotions, or anything else, you are ignoring the real and sticking yourself into time and meaning and separateness. You can no more "let go" than you could make that lovely experience happen to begin with! Everything happens, and the false me-identity says, I did it! Or, it happened to ME! That is the ignorance; mind is focused on a mistake, an entity that believes IT is the doer and knower ... and ignores the space that this mind-identity occurs in; that space of your True-Nature of Being, the unbounded pure non-conceptual awake awareness, which is utterly clear, empty, transparent, and both unattainable and unavoidable. It's NOT a thing and yet, IT IS. Ungraspable unknowable Isness. One-Essence of Being, Consciousness, Peace.

Q: I had another experience which is easier to see as unrealistic and that's when on a walk I suddenly was bathed in powerful unconditional love, everything including me was that love - wow. Of course that was over quickly and now only a faint memory......... But quite often I feel that subtle bubbly joy within me (caused by nothing) and it feels more like something real than an experience since it seems to be there all the time. I just don't notice it when I am involved with something but it is there under the surface - just a mirage, perhaps?

C. Yes, a mirage you might out of force of a bad habit still believe will yield water to quench your thirst ... someday! All ignoring the truth of simply being, empty and spacelike. Beginningless and endless, UNBORN.

Q: I still identify with my body, I tend to breath shallow and then when the thought appears "I breath shallow - better breath more deeply", I do so - feel better, and that re-enforces my belief that I control the well being of my body. Or, I had arrhythmia which was fixed with surgery, however I still have benign heart beat hiccups which are caused by stress (according to my cardiologist) and when they occur I believe that I could decrease these events with certain 'actions' - like calming myself etc. But that's all crap - however it has a grip on me.

C. Okay, take that assumption that there is an "I" with a name and it is the controller. Now USE that control to NOT have the shallow breath happen in the first place! You'll quickly see in your own experience that control is absolutely an illusion. Test it for yourself and the proof is in the direct seeing that our attempts to control always ultimately fail! Moreover, it is only when something unwanted has ALREADY arisen that the attempt to be responsible and take charge, to take over control, happens. Also what gets IGNORED in this is that there IS a Power that makes it all appear; makes the Sun burn, beats the heart, creates air for all the bodies to breathe. Where IS that Source? WHAT is That? ARE you controlling that Source? Or is this me idea just a thought appearing and being animated BY that Source, like a toaster is animated by electricity? Think on these pointers. Look deep within the space and see if you can find a "me that is the driver" of that car called you. Knowing "it's all crap" is NOT going to set you free. Find out what this "knower" actually IS. Does it exist? Does it REALLY control anything? All you can do is watch. This watching-seeing awareness is arising as the awake-witnessing-consciousness and That is incontrovertibly real. Stay with I AM; that I AM is undeniable. YOU ARE and that I that I AM, and that I that You are, ARE the Nondual One I of Being, awake and alive, happening forever as the Energy driving everything. All that is and all that is not is only That...

Q: That's it for now. My best to you

C. And you. Have a great now.

66. I AM ... Stop right here! :-)

Q: I Am ...

Stop right here!

...a seeker of over 20 years with meditation practices and living in a spiritual community (for about 4 years) and ending up with non-duality.

Ahhhh you didn't stop! Now we hear The Familiar Seeker Story!

Q: It is exhilarating and very frustrating for me at the same time and even the teachers like Ramesh, Gangaji, Wayne Liquorman, John Wheeler, Tony Parsons, etc. are sometimes contradicting themselves.

C. The mind sees contradiction where what is actually arising is PARADOX. The essence of the paradox of nonduality is that a) there is no person and b) so long as there is the assumption, the belief, that you are a person inquiry is advised. While in truth there is no person, until that is the Being-Actuality and NOT merely a belief in being no-one, some intervention so advised by those who have seen the Real and discarded the false and are encouraging you to do the same in various ways unique to the particular organism's expression of the inexpressible. In my view all those you name are in this category. SIT with the paradox. Be with this paradox. Don't try to resolve it; let it sit there like a brick in your lap. See what crumbles as this is sat with so to speak. It is an old pointer that the guardians at the gateless gate of Truth are Paradox and Confusion. Confusion is NOT KNOWING. Be in Not Knowing. Be with the Paradox.

John Wheeler's books (and others) just always bring it back to our true nature, beyond the mind and time and any concepts. Back to the basics, "WHO YOU ARE - I AM. Just THAT"

Who am I? Who are you? I AM. That is Consciousness, Knowing-Aliveness. Look with the question, WHAT am I? What is it that I take myself to be? Who do you consider your self to be? The truth is you are not this, not that, not any object, not a knower, not an object known. You as Awareness are

Naked Natural Knowing. Life, LIFE-ING. Moving Energy-Aliveness. This is everything out of nothing. Nothing Being Everything. NOT TWO.

Q: You recommended Tony Parsons' book "Nothing Being Everything" which is great but also deflated 'my' notion that 'I' really could do something about it – who is saying "Who Am I" when there is only an appearance which is simply outplaying some genetic programming? There is no volition but simply happenings with no or a result – and that result is a Fata Morgana collapsing – LOL.

C. It's all done with mirrors. What you see "out there" is an image in the mirror that is paradoxically (again!) an image OF the mirror … an image (imagination) of The Self (Being-Awareness-Aliveness.) And to "know" or believe that there is no-one and to BE that there is no-one are as is said over and over here, night and day apart!

Q: What is the difference between inquiring "Who Am I" and to just go on with life and if the curtain falls – fine, if not – just as fine?

C. The question is, where IS any "controlling personal entity" with the volition or will to choose or decide to do either!? Can you find one in direct actual experience? Only when you take a thought to be what you are is there this false notion of the doer. All happens by itself. Realization that what is, is and what is not, is not, and … so what!? is a natural happening, like breathing. To paraphrase The Buddha, actions happen, deeds are done, and in truth there is no individual doer, not in you nor in anyone else. Life Happening! Wonderful! Onederful!

Q: This mind is, of course, freaked out by the notion that our true nature is not me, but some 'strange' no-thing – yikes!

C. The mind, which is nothing but a false assumption that there is an "I" or "me" apart from Totality, is terrified to be faced with its insignificance, its emptiness and meaninglessness. That IS its inauthenticity. And fearing the emptiness is another flip strategy the false ego employs to keep emptiness at bay by turning it on itself and making up the meaning that emptiness is about "me" and "I" do NOT want to be empty and meaningless, because that seeing in a way invalidates "my whole life" (and especially "my" noble search for God!) It IS … YOU ARE … Empty and Meaningless, and it's empty and meaningless that it's empty and meaningless. This is known by no-one and cannot be either attained OR lost.

WHO does all that? Do YOU control that happening? If this is YOU why don't you just call a halt to this being freaked out? Seeing that you are powerless to change anything (because by the time "you" show up as a thought the happening is already over and all that is left is a memory and you might well be taking this memory of a self that acted to be who you are.)

Q: This morning, in the process of waking up, there was the – how do I put it – knowledge of that there is only space, emptiness and anything else faded away, and then of course the mind cheerfully chimed in "to make sense of it" – LOL.

C. That is what happens. This is the seeing and then the attempt by the false "knower" to gain and grasp and own. No worries. Just witness it. You ARE the Witnessing Consciousness that is seeing and knowing. Being that suffering dries up and you remain as you always are, the Unborn Naked Being-Awareness of Aliveness, LIFE living itself through that organism.

BEING, Your Real Being, is (metaphorically) an empty mind and a full heart.

Suffering and questions end in the seeing that the "I" has never existed. Do not chase down questions and try to figure it out in the mind. If you want to look at anything, see how all problems and doubts are for the "I". Then have a look at the "I". There is no "I", only non-conceptual awareness here, there and everywhere. In this, life flows — the heart beats, the breath moves. Thoughts, feelings, actions happen spontaneously and effortlessly in the space of awareness. Pause and experience how easy it all is. How much work are "you" doing to beat your heart, generate a thought and so on? So relax and do whatever comes up to do in the energy of awareness. See what I am saying and you will not need any further pointers. You will experience all this for yourself.

- John Wheeler

67. You ARE That Being-Awakeness-Peace

Q: Earlier yesterday morning I had a sort of 'awakening' experience... different from my previous experiences in that I can only think of it as an increased purity of consciousness. Previously I would characterize my experiences as movements of energy within my body which brought me temporary peace but ultimately had no effect on the issue of the ego. I have been contemplating the question of 'Who am I?' for every waking moment that I've not been focused on something else... and I notice that when I get in touch with that deeper sense of 'I am' all anger, anxiety, worry, etc seem to disappear, and I feel a sort of pleasant calmness.

C. This calmness, this Perfect Peace, IS what You are.

Q: I'm slowly realizing that my mind constructs everything around me... and that most moments of my life have been spent deeply absorbed in the mind, "asleep" to the greater reality around me. I feel like I'm moving closer towards that state of unobstructed awakeness. Thanks :)

C. This sounds good. Now: Just see that in actuality that "unobstructed awakeness" is already always here now, just overlooked. This Being-Awakeness-Peace NEVER comes and goes. All that we call me and world appears, changes, and disappears on the screen of Being-Awakeness-Peace. YOU ARE THAT. There is no attaining That nor can you ever LOSE That. The investigation, looking into who am I? is a divine energy of the True Self that is simply removing the false, that seeming "obstruction," which is what overlooks or ignores the real. It will not happen someday. It is what is right NOW. There is no time unless you think and believe there is a separateness in the whole. This is the matrix of thought ... time-space-location-twoness, me and other. You are this inescapable I AM, and that is the real. Stay with that simple I AM and look, being I AM as you are looking with the final unanswerable question who am I? ... just that. Simple. This is Love. Stay in touch ... I love you as The Self of All Beings.

Words are an obvious problem; so don't get hung up on them. There is nothing that needs to be done or practiced. Just notice that it is always now. See that time is really a thing of the mind. Because the focus is in the mind you miss the immediacy and the freshness of now.

- John Greven

68. Beyond Being, BE

A pal shares a poem by the poet-saint "Akha" ...

Avoid "I," beyond body be,

Swim in the Lord's flowing stream.

One who has lost "I" and "me,"

Mingles easy in His sea.

Akha, have insight this way,

Space is in the center every which way

This is AWE Fully Good

All the seeking, all the spiritual practices, and all the effort to understand veils the plain and simple truth of this, as it is. Whatever thought arises, whatever feeling comes up, be it labeled good or bad, there is something still and quietly aware of all that's going on. It simply is, without the slightest effort. Snap your fingers. Did you hear the sound? How much effort did that take? None! Now, at this very moment, Pure Awareness is the silent background to you reading these words. You don't have to do a thing for it to be there. It is always present, even though it is too close to get at, like the eye is too close to see itself.

-Leo Hartong

69. "I Am Awake"

Follow-up from J.H. - A 3 part mini-note. Loved your warm, gentle & wise response in "How Do I Do the Investigation?" Sometimes a gentle bell & sometimes a giant gong. Both useful tools.

C. That is how it worked for me. Slammed up-against-the-ego-wall by some, lovingly embraced and guided by some. And they all had only the freedom of a friend at stake. (Before I get attacked by The Advaita Police, yes there is no I and no other AND as long as it seems that there are me and other, then… it seems that there's me and others! So what? No problem with that unless a judging ego thinks there is. Ha!) Anyway …

Q: Trying to track the empty it's through the streets of my imagination. Who Am I/ Who is j.h.? It seems like something has flipped over or reversed. Realization of Presence Awareness (I don't know how else to try to communicate the "experience") as both Who I truly Am and the constant Background/Source of It All is with "me" much of the time. The background music shape shifts into All and Everything. Ah Yes.

C. You express this really eloquently!

Q: Part 3 is just to say Hi. It feels good to stay in contact. (I know, "to whom") Sometimes it's like picking a path through a mine field and sometimes its joyful relief and peace. Comin' Home.

C. Yes, and THAT is all that matters. Not the opinion of "fundamentalist non-dualists," not the naysayers that it's all hopeless (though of course it IS a hope for a better more powerful 'me' that keeps the appearance of bondage happening! This is so paradoxical!) As you see now, there is what IS and That is beyond describing, beyond sentience, beyond perceiving, like a camera lens that registers all that appears in it's field of vision with no evaluation, no labels, and no emotional attachment. All is as it is and allowed by the no-one that we are in Truth … and now you have come to see that this Home is the abode you never actually left. Awake in the dream, this, to paraphrase a friend, Leo Hartong, is Being Awake to the fact of the dream-nature of what appears. Being, Awake AS What Is … Changeless Being, Choiceless Awareness. So, welcome HOME! And clearly all is well in The Unborn Being we are. The gift of Unknowing is as Leo says, "The Gift Of Lucid Living."

According to legend, a seeker asked The Buddha, "Who are you?" The Buddha answered, "I am awake." Now you are the Buddha … but of course you always were. Everyone is Already Awake. Cool! Many thanks for sharing the Good News! Love ya … c.

70. How Do I DO the Investigation?

Who Asks That Question?

Quite a few have asked, essentially, "HOW do I DO this investigation? Do I just ask who am I over and over? I have tried that, it seems to reveal a sense of space and openness but soon I am right back into the pain of being me, and I am still suffering. This goes on in spite of years of commitment to being earnest and taking up practices and meditations etc. I am tired of flopping back into being a little complaining me and I want to end this search for real. What to do? How to see that the I is a phantom as is pointed out by these Nondual teachings?"

The "pat answer" in Nonduality circles is to ask, WHO wants to know? That is a great pointer for some but for many it just increases the frustration and is often dismissed as "fundamentalism" or "Advaita-speak" and is certainly NOT helpful in those cases. It's almost kind of condescending...

I can share that the two things that helped the most for me were the seeing that this that I am is not a concept or experience but a silent open background of space-like awareness that is always here before anything else and that I am that awareness. As Bob Adamson and John Wheeler reminded me, we START from that simple undeniable fact that, undeniably, I exist, I AM.

That led to a clear seeing that I AM what I was seeking. Then there came a dropping back into self-identification, self-centered (selfish) thoughts, and the space of simply being appeared to be lost again. That was painful! Then the need for a real down and dirty investigation challenging the mind and its false concepts and assumptions became evident as the suffering … painful emotions and unwanted intense experiences of feeling sad, contracted, angry, frustrated etc. happened again and again.

Something I found very helpful was listening to Stephen Wingate talk about his own experience of this, and how our mutual friend John Wheeler had guided him to make the investigation personal and real in his own experience. In Stephen's case, as he shares, he began asking himself new questions, along the lines of what exactly IS "Stephen?" He was looking into his own experience of being alive instead of applying a "one size fits all" generic pointer. This did the trick for Stephen (you can hear him discuss in detail how specifically this happened on his excellent audio CDs.)

So I started looking in these more direct personal ways, with support from many friends, including Bob, John, John Greven, Stephen, and Annette Nibley. It is GREAT to have friends like these along the seeking path!

I started looking more deeply at what or who IS this "Charlie" person, what is it that I really believe I am? Several things, identities if you like, came up, and were tested for "truth." What I found is that the mind makes endless assertions about what I am and when I fail to seek evidence for its assertions I leave the false unchallenged ... and that leaves the cause of suffering in place and it continues to create havoc for this boy's life!

For example: I am "Charles in charge." I am "the boss." I am "the actor, the doer, the decider." I am "me" and you are "not me." "I am me and the way things work around here is we do things MY way." It's "My way or the highway." And so on. The I am as an identity that Charlie is, is bossy, arrogant and knows everything about everything. "I Am what I think and I am right" was another one. A know-it-all. But all these fail the truth test. I am always finding out I don't know about something. There is always a clear failure to "make life go my way" ... over and over! Wanting things to go my way is as effective as telling the weather not to rain. Or trying to herd cats.

But that was all a sort of "array of branches" and the root still had not been gotten down to. So the looking into this space of being I show up in for some root cause went on for a while. Then it became clear that "I am the one who is looking for what I am." "I must find out what I am." This arises as a sense of frustration as there seems to be a power to think, I can choose what thoughts to focus my attention on, however, while I CAN choose a created thought like "Who Am I?" what I have NO control over is that power that causes thinking itself to arise! It happens! Thoughts happen, whether I want them to or not! In other words I can select from a menu of thoughts so to say, BUT I cannot choose to have NO thoughts come up. And I saw that experience follows concept, that a thought of me that thinks leads to the idea that I can choose and decide and have it my way, and the frustration of trying to practice choice and having my choices be thwarted is really painful. The mind intends for example to never get upset again because I know that when I get upset it hurts, and it's unhealthy etc. BUT the next time I am triggered by some happening that is not in accordance with what I intend, bang! I am in a tantrum, like a bratty kid, cussing at myself for (again) overeating and getting fat, or (again) dropping something and berating myself for being clumsy, etc.

So what this showed me is that for me, who I am is "a stupid idiot who STILL can't do anything right. Despite all these years of experience and practice, I am still at the effect of some mechanism that runs me and makes me still believe 'I am me' and that 'me' is an old, clumsy, stupid, angry person."

So I came back to what Stephen was pointing out and looked into this more deeply than ever: What IS Charlie? What actually IS Charles? What IS "this person, here?" This "me" is subtler than a thought, finer than an experience, less evident than the surface stuff described above. What IS Charles?

Finally the seeing arose, "I don't know!"

Abiding as this "I don't Know" brought the mind to a full stop and there was and is what was sought … Perfect Peace, Absolute Freedom. Timeless Choiceless Awareness, like a blank clear transparent screen on which apparent choices and chooser arise together; on which the apparent opposites of I and other arise together. THAT, I AM. THAT, THOU ART.

This is inquiry: the key as far as I can tell is the "making it real for me." Making it about my own experience instead of someone else's, because no Guru or Friend can be alive for me, no one else experiences life as I experience it, so it really HAD to become directly and personally MY looking. The guidance from friends like John and Stephen that were complete in their search was invaluable, yet in the final analysis it was up to me.

And so, the final truth is clear and self-evident: I AM That I AM. Being, Choiceless Awareness ... Just That and Nothing Else.

Finding your own path into this inquiry may take some new and fresh personal ways to look into yourself for yourself. Te website and my books are here to support that looking for yourself, by yourself, as are the friends listed on my website links page.

I love you all as my own Self, and of course I wish you the very best. Thanks for taking time to read this. I hope it helps, if you are still suffering.

71. Who Thinks 'I'm a Seeker'?

Q: I am what you can call a spiritual seeker. But I have a question that I can't resolve in my mind and that causes a lot of confusion. It has to do with other people. To me it seems almost strange that there are so many people and different forms. I can't explain it very well but it's like it's not normal to me-like it seems to be for others- that there can be so many different human forms. For example when I am in a crowded area I am almost overwhelmed because of all these people. Now I have read in spiritual books and so that all humanity is actually one person and that an other person is actually you. Can you say something about this? Thank you very much and all the best.

C. First off you say I am … what you can call a spiritual seeker etc. – that is a false identification! Stop at I AM. The I AM is the only true and certain thing you can know about yourself. All that FOLLOWS I am is false. Lies!

Secondly we do NOT say there is only one "person"! The apparent persons are certainly separate and appear AS individual body-mind organisms! What is pointed to is there is only one I AM. This I AM is NOT a "person" or any "thing" at all. This presence, that is aware there where you are, is the timeless I Am-ness that is PRIOR to language and has NO separate "identity".

This is the essence of it: Being IS and there is no escape from That, nor any possibility of attaining That. You ARE.

Can you deny that this Isness IS obviously Present and Aware, open, empty and clear? It is the most available and undeniable space. IT IS. That was never lost. You are That. That's all there is to this - Seeing what was never absent and always completely free. That is the universal I AM that I AM and YOU ARE.

That's IT.

Follow-up: Thank you!

C. It's all done with mirrors.

The freedom I point to has nothing to do with awakening, enlightenment, or liberation. It has no steps or stages, either before or after such illusory events. Such attainments are purely conceptual and have no reality at all. How can there be pre-requisites or follow up stages if there is no special event or attainment involved? I point to the ever-present, ever-attained sense of "I am", that sense of being and knowing which naturally shines within you right now. Furthermore, that "I am" sense itself comes and goes as a time-bound state. Seeing this much, it is evident that even now you are the unborn, uncreated, timeless source of all that is. No special awakenings are needed, because this is a simple, present fact. The separate self or "I" entity is a fiction. Therefore, there is no one present to carry out or be interested in any intricacies after so-called "awakening". Such is the glorious natural yoga shared by Nisargadatta Maharaj with those who met him, such as Bob Adamson and others. This natural yoga is brilliant and all comprehensive. Fortunate are those who recognize its value.

- John Wheeler

Yes Indeed!

72. Under The Rainbow

So, how does this search end?
Where does it all lead?
Do you REALLY wanna know my friend
Do you really wanna see?

Well, my child...
I think you already do

Deep down, somewhere

i think you always knew
in the end, when nothing's left
and you finally face your fear
standing there, well not for long
you'll start to disappear
you see, the self can never reach
a place that's so secure

'cause all it has is nothingness
of which it can't endure

but as you start to fade away
nothing could be wrong
now, you can fully play
laugh and sing a song

you can still be angry too
or even sadness you can sing
because that is not really you
it's all just Love happening

 - J.A.

Beautiful! And very clear.
Love! –c

73. What Is The Source of SOURCE?

Follow-up: I mentally register what you are saying and am open to the idea of non-existence... I have had many moments of 'mental blankness' in which thought-activity is clear and I feel a sense of peace and contentment. Yet I do not feel what may be characterized as a deep, eternal peace and unity with all existence. It is rather frustrating. Should I meditate? Look harder/deeper for the sense of 'I am?' Train myself to be more focused?

C. Just keep looking for the separate person. Asking WHO AM I? - do not take any answer! Apart from a thought or feeling, that comes and goes, is it there? What you REALLY are IS EMPTY - beyond description. All you as an entity are is memory and imagination. Stay with this. Other than a natural sense of curiosity, asking that me who are you? there is really nothing needed. just be as you are – No Thing.

Q: Thank you so much. I'm beginning to understand. There is the ego, and there is awareness. The ego clouds awareness yet is also a part of awareness. Within awareness there is joy and aliveness and life beyond description... it reminds me of when I go skydiving. I glimpsed it today. Now it is just a matter of deepening. Thank you thank you thank you :)...

C. You are very welcome. If you like, contemplate this pointer: Something says "I AM." What IS that? Something knows, "I AM." What IS that? LOOK directly at the thought "I". What is that? What is the SOURCE of that thought? LOOK directly into the sense of being, being alive, being awake. What IS that? What is the SOURCE of that? Do you know? WHAT knows? What is the SOURCE of knowing? Do you know that you do NOT know? What is the SOURCE of that NOT knowing? What is the Source of SOURCE? What are you? Challenge the thinker-mind, what ARE you? LOOK out at "the world." ASK that world WHAT ARE YOU? What ARE You!? WHERE did you come from? WHERE are you going?

Watch the mind answer. Ask that thinker-storyteller, WHAT ARE YOU? WHERE did you come from? WHERE are you going? WHAT makes you happen? WHAT is the SOURCE of you? Are you REAL? WHAT says yes? What says NO? What ARE You!? WHERE did you come from? WHERE are you going?

What IS the Source of IS? What IS ... "IS" ... ?

NO ANSWER will satisfy. ONLY "No Answer."

74. Is This It?

Follow-up Q: Sunday, this body-mind took a bath after listening on-line to one of the conference calls you so graciously linked to in your newsletter. After doing some progressive relaxation exercises, I began asking the question: "What Am I, Really?" There was a noticing in the space that opened up between the questions, of a sense of ever deepening peacefulness and serenity, the likes of which I had never known. It reminded one of the calm surface of a pool of water but with an unspoken sense of awareness and deep knowing. Passing thoughts could not cause so much as a ripple on its surface. The thoughts and mental noise came and went, but this deep serenity persisted unscathed.   There was the awareness that it has always been present, just obscured by all the rantings and ravings of the ego-mind. It felt like "home".

This was very different from the "everyday awareness" that is usually experienced, but it seemed hidden in the background, under everything (for lack of a better description.) It definitely was not a "state", and seemed quite genuine and real. The mood for the rest of the day was elated, although this deep knowing and serenity seemed to slip to the background once more.

Is that some of what is being pointed to, or just an artifact of deep relaxation upon awareness?

C. That was an experience that arose on the empty screen of the Being that you are. So yes in that as a pointer it can be a kind of sample but ultimately NO in that NO experience is "it".

YOU are It. You cannot attain or experience what you are. The experiencing is the actual; the experiencer is false.

Ponder that while seeing that you ARE and that is the real!

75. How To Stay In Awareness - I AM?

J.H. Writes, Listened to our "Hardball II" conversation MP3 and your "Chat with Sergio" today. Question: Awareness of I AM seems to be the key that unlocks the door that isn't really there. Staying with the Awareness I AM seems to be so simple, pure and natural. But then along comes an identification with some event or aspect of "the story" and whoosh a trap door seems to open into the jungle of thought and confusion. No light in that jungle. A complete "forgetting." Round and round I go trying to see and sort it out (suffering) until finally I give up (Surrender). That Surrender seems to lead back into the light.

C. And ALL of that happens in this Presence of Awareness. This Awareness is NOT a "thing" that comes and goes. IT IS. And this Isness registers all the comings and goings of thoughts, sensations, identifications with a story, feelings, sensations … sentience appears in That and THAT is what NEVER changes. You cannot escape That. IT IS, Being-Awareness-Aliveness, present and clear prior to and during and after all movements of thoughts feelings etc. Surrender? Who is there to do that? Dissolution of the false happens when there arises an investigation into the nature of the I or me we have mistakenly taken our self to be.

Q: How to stay in the Awareness of I AM and let the story flow?

C. You cannot escape that. Wanting to "stay in That" is happening IN that. It is like water to the fish: So clear and obvious that it is overlooked (but the analogy falls short because Awareness, unlike water, is NOT a thing you can grasp or know.) Awareness is the Silence of Stillness knowing; the knower and known are illusions arising IN that Being-Awake-And-Aware Aliveness that is the Real. THAT is non-conceptual and therefore cannot be grasped by the "I" which is itself only another concept. That I can never "know Oneness." You are NOT that I-thought which tries to stay with I AM. Being IS and that you are. Attempting to stay in That is a flip strategy for avoiding That.

76. A Mind Is Telling Itself Stories Again

Follow-up: Thank you for your reply, Charlie. I too agree that there are no teachers of this, but it sure does seem that way! Maybe that is the paradox I suppose! I think it's my mind telling stories again!!

C. Exactly!

Q: Yes, only awakeness, and it's not personal, I like the way you say that. Haha, and you didn't use too many "quotation marks", well done! :-) But still Charlie I would say that you DO seem to be becoming more and more of a teacher. I don't mean that as a criticism, more of a worrying observation! Is there any desire for you to be teaching this stuff? Surely that desire disappears when this is seen? Anyway, thanks for listening. That "quote unquote" stuff is really unnecessary though, but then again, if it makes you happy! Do what you do my friend, it's all okay here! :-) Love you too.

C. There is absolutely NO desire here to teach or share. All desire to teach died when I died. This sharing HAPPENS. No-one teaches. Some are moved by Energy-Aliveness to share ... Tony Parsons, for example. Bob Adamson. John Wheeler. A few others. This just happens! Like breathing happens. There is no chooser or doer here or anywhere; that is a false belief. What dies is the belief in separation and choice. If I had a choice I would most likely just sleep, meditate, eat, watch TV, eat, chase women, eat, get drunk, eat, sleep. I could give a shit if no-one ever writes or calls again. When there is asking there is sharing. All happens by itself. When no-one writes there is no sharing. So far there's sharing. It could stop today and never happen again! Who pretends to know? Not I.

My question for you is, who CARES what happens through this charlie thing? What makes you "be concerned?" What's driving you to think, to write, to breathe? Find THAT and all questions die as there can only be a question like this when there is questioner ... a belief in individuals with choice and volition. This IS the paradox: There is no person and the appearing person shares. Not Two. I don't "take it as criticism." There is no person to do that, not here and not there. Nothing "makes me happy." There is happiness here, as well as sadness, grief, joy... all happening in the Bliss of the I AM that I AM and YOU ARE! I Love You as That I Am. Stay with THAT. I AM... that is all.

(That all said, on the "relative" level, thanks for your friendship and love!)

77. There Are No Teachers Of This

Q: I have recently been watching your YouTube videos and looking at your website. There is some nice stuff on there, but please, one thing bothers me. Could you stop saying "quote unquote" all the time, and putting quotation marks "around" "every" "single" "word" "you" "use"? It seems you are trying so hard to be properly "nondualistic". Charlie, you really don't need to try so hard!! And I know "you" (see how annoying it is?) will say that "you" are not doing it. But really Charlie, you can just write normally if you want to. Stop trying to be a teacher, you used to be so much better and more authentic months ago when you admitted that you were not enlightened and were just a normal person. These days you are trying so hard (and it shows!) to teach. There are no teachers of THIS!

C. Thanks for writing! The expression that comes out here happens in response to e-mails and phone calls that come here and it seems to me that there needs to be these kinds of emphasis. If it appears there is someone trying to teach, then that's how you see it. I don't experience it that way. And I feel strongly that I am NOT "an enlightened person;" there is NO such thing in Reality. Not Ramana not Bob not Tony not any "meat." There is only already awakeness and that ain't personal. So ... It's all a wondrous dream and that includes ... well, everything. Even this. So anyway thanks again for sharing your view! For the record [:-)] ... I completely agree that there are NO teachers of This ... ALL There IS, IS This as-it-is, and That is That.

I Love you.

Paradoxically the mystery is also pure simplicity, or an open secret. It is everything perceived, as well as the perceiving itself. It is not something the mind can grasp, but the mind can realize its own limitations here and let go. At this instant it can be understood that there is no one to understand. What remains is simply understanding; not the understanding OF the mystery, but of Being AS the mystery.

-Leo Hartong

78. The Impersonal I AM Is BLISS

Q: Ramana Maharshi says that Awareness is existence, consciousness, bliss. Are you always blissful?

C. Yes, and so are YOU. (The REAL YOU.)

I AM IS Existence-BEING, Consciousness AWARENESS, Bliss-PEACE.

I AM IS Bliss. I AM IS Impersonal and Eternal. Absolute Freedom.

YES, I am THAT. And, dear One, so are "YOU."

The ONE I AM is ALL.

79. ONLY Love Is Real and That Thou Art

H.R. Writes, I was in tears hearing your conversation with Paul... his laughter is bursting with love and joy, innocence, aliveness itself!!! Did you know [my name] means freedom? Your love is so freeing! "I" love the fact that you are in my life...

C. This is beautiful! Love frees the seeker from its false assumptions and does that effortlessly! And there is NO doer, only Love is Real and you ARE That... You are not "your name" ... as the Real You knows and IS ... always. You ARE Freedom. You are love. Love IS Freeing no-one. I AM is ever-fresh and Already FREE! I AM is Freedom. Be that and Nothing Else, dear One. I AM Life. Now it's known in [that-name]-Freedom: I AM LIFE ItSelf.... and it takes One to "know" I AM ... One.

Love from I AM to I AM! (Apologies if this is preaching at the choir!)

80. What Never Changes Wherever You Are?

G.H. writes, Hello! I enjoy your YouTube videos, and have actually had a few moments of 'present-ness' and freedom from mind while watching them, one which occurred several minutes ago but disappeared just as a wave recedes from the shore of a beach.

C. That's what some call "free samples." Yet they are NOT what is being pointed to. These experiences ALWAYS come to pass and not to stay. What is it that registers the arising and passing of that experience? What never changes?

Q: For about 9 months now I have been practicing 'looking within' at the 'doer' by trying to become as aware as possible of the physical sensations within my body. When I do this, however, I feel a sort of emotional pressure in my solar plexus region which intensifies as I stay aware of it. If I focus on it enough, my body literally starts to shake and convulse.

C. Where exactly IS this "I" – "I" – "I" you refer to? What do you assume your self to be? This "I" thought: does it have any power to create, change or fix WHAT IS? Practices can and usually do obscure the obviousness of Being-Awakeness-Aliveness that You, in essence, are.

Q: My neck becomes tense and my shoulders involuntarily shrug up. After these convulsions, however, I experience a sort of clear-headedness and lightness of mind which goes away as I return to my daily activities and routines. Have you heard of anyone experiencing this on their journey to becoming awakened? If so, what's the best way to deal with it? Thanks.

C. Yes. Anything can happen. Many seekers who practice "kundalini" or have had some "initiation" or "shaktipat diksha" experience such things. But they mean absolutely NOTHING. ALL experiences simply come and go in Awareness. YOU are AWARENESS and NOT a concept or an experience … those are things and You are No Thing. Being, just THAT. I AM.

This stuff all happens all by itself… to NO-one. Then the mind (which is an assumed entity made up of the belief in an "I" and "time") makes up meaning where none actually exists. To ask how to "deal with it" ASSUMES, incorrectly, that there IS a person, a controlling "me-entity called 'I'" that could exert some force of will or control. Look in the space where you are. There is I AM ... Being-Awareness ... and that is all. Seek the actual solid personal will that could change what appears in the Space of Being and you always always always come up empty-handed. But only ALWAYS!

You are the Pure I AM of Being-Awakeness, witnessing presence ... Consciousness IS and you are THAT. And your TRUE Empty nature is That which IS and Prior to Consciousness ... like Deep Sleep as a metaphor ... Being IS and before Awakeness. "Darkness within darkness, the gateway to all mystery" as Lao Tzu put it. Ultimately you are this blank emptiness which paradoxically also appears and loves to be appearing as ALL THAT IS.

This is what you are: Unborn, loving, spacelike Being. Don't believe this! Look for the "I" that seems or feels separate from The Whole and it is clear that seeing is, and there is no "person" doing that. There never was; it was only a dream!

Stay in touch. Love from I AM to I AM,

81. De Nada

S.G. Follows up with, J I see, all what happens is apparent. always was and is that way. And the "I Am" is the only secure, the only unchangeable. What a simplicity. No one to save, yes, this is freedom. :) I admire that solvency, that stability to Remain as Your Self. And in your case be capable of point it directly. Many thanks Master ... You say you are a friend, yes, the Master is that I Am ;-) that is the only I Am ... After our phone chat ... What a silence, a tangible silence .... is so fantastic. Really. Wow. Thanks.

C. Excellent ... stay put in That! Your MP3 link is attached here.

There is NO student NO Master. Only THIS: I AM. De Nada!

Q: It's like I don't sleep..... and nothings happens really. Like stay in the same "place" "all the time" and nothing happens there. Wonderful.

C. Welcome HOME.

82. Love Is Home

Recognize ... "The Tao that can be told is not the eternal Tao. The name that can be named is not the eternal name. The nameless is the beginning of heaven and earth..." –*Lao Tzu*

Love is my name for the nameless.

The mind is clearly an appearance that comes and goes as an experience to you. So the mind has about zero percent to do with any of this. What the mind appears to (which is you) is both present and aware. This is completely obvious and beyond doubt. Even a doubt about it requires that you are present and aware to perceive the doubt. So just settle down right here with your doubtless sense of knowing and being. Get to know this present nature that you already are.

- John Wheeler

83. What Should Happen?

Q: I can find a blankness, a space between the thoughts. And this space is this "no-one looking", right? But to stay there, in that space between those thoughts, is for me impossible...

C. Of course it is impossible "for me." Because this "me" is an appearance IN blank empty no-thing. Space IS and that is what You are. Not the "you" that tries and fails to "stay there" - the YOU of Blank Empty Space-Like Meaninglessness! All of this seeing, asking questions, wanting to know "how" - who is doing that? What is making "you" think and write and do anything? What is in charge? What wakes you up, makes you BE? That blankness between thoughts is NOT the Empty Being-Awareness that is Real. That blankness is an appearance IN the Real Absolute No Thing which is paradoxically also Everything. Sit still with this. If questions arise, ask, who asks this? If doubts arise, ask, who doubts? Who is this me? Where is this "I"- asker? You True nature is Empty Meaningless Space, and That is the Fullness of Absolute Freedom, Absolute Acceptance, Absolutely NOTHING but Unconditional Non-conceptual LOVE. Sit with all this.

Q: What exactly is it that should happen?

C. NOTHING.

84. "Knowing" Does Not End Suffering!

M.L. writes, I'd like to tell you what's been happening here the last couple of months. First off, I had a profound experience when I was asleep. I suddenly became fully conscious and could hear myself snoring - or rather just a body snoring, like it wasn't even my body, could've been anyone's. It was blissfully peaceful, but came and went.

C. It's not an uncommon "spiritual experience." Meditators generally make a big deal out of these, as the experience of "witnessing sleep" is thought to be a signpost that the seeker is "close to final enlightenment." That is of course merely another "spiritual myth." There a zillion of them, and this one is pretty popular. The same thing was experienced here, a few years ago; "I" found "myself" watching the body sleep and hearing it snore. The bad news is, this means absolutely nothing! It's just another experience (though not a relatively common one for most folks) that ... guess what ... comes and goes! As you realized. The focus on experiences and blissful moods is a real distraction from the core essence of Nonduality, which points out that what you actually are is NOT an experience, NOT an experiencer, NOT a "personal witnesser"... what you are never changes, not ever. That Awareness- Consciousness is the witnessing Awaring unknowable knowing and THAT is beyond knower and known. Prior to all concepts and all experiences Awareness IS ... this observing-consciousness is ALWAYS what's so and who you are; it is simply ignored because it is utterly ordinary and WAY too simple and obvious! This is NOT a thing that the mind-thought or ego-sense of the separate "personal me" can grasp or gain. THE I-Concept POINTS to PURE AWARENESS. That is Unbounded, empty, self-luminous. THAT THOU ART. Unborn Being.

The ULTIMATE paradox is this: You are Nothing ... and That is Everything!

This can never be found and never be held onto, AND This can never be lost! It is the Being that you are. And there is NO way out of Being. Kill the body, Being is still present and absolutely unmoved and untouched! You cannot kill your Self. No shit. You cannot kill space. How could you annihilate No Thing?

Q: A couple of weeks later I felt like I was visited by the devil. It happened when I was asleep again, although I didn't know I was asleep because in the dream I was lying awake in my bed. Suddenly there was a hurricane in my bedroom and a wind pinning me down on my bed. It was really intense and scary and went on for ages. A few weeks after that, I had an 'episode' where I felt an intense joy bubbling up in me, and couldn't stop giggling. This too came and went.

C. A waking dream... or nightmare? Daymare? All hallucination. Not all hallucinations are drug induced. Anything can appear. ANYTHING. Question is, what does that all appear IN? Were you NOT Being? Was Awareness gone? Awareness is the only constant unchanging featureless empty space ... like the cinema screen. That said, there may be a chemical element here. Have you seen a physician? There might be a cellular imbalance that can be corrected with medications. It sounds a bit like bipolar disorder the way you describe it.

By the way suicidal thoughts are often a byproduct of this kind of "mechanistic' disorder. If the car isn't running right take it to a good mechanic. In my view, that is what doctors are ... mechanics for the car, the bodymind apparatus.

In any event, this is all a bunch of waking dreams. Some "preferable" to others perhaps. BUT ALL THAT IS WHAT APPEARS AND NOT WHAT IS ULTIMATELY REAL. YOU ARE UNBORN. Only an idea of a me gets born and dreams and giggles maniacally, or shits its britches in fear.

Q: I know that 'I' am not in control of any of these things that happen or will happen. I know that I don't think my own thoughts any more than I digest my own food.

C. Those pointers are accurate in a way BUT: When that is something "you know" that is the bullshit false knowledge of an identity. When you say "I know," what is revealed is that you believe all this crap rather than asking that believer, who are you? Where is the believer? What is making thoughts arise that say "I know," OR "I don't know?" Infinite Energetic alive beingness is this livingness arising as all that appears and the knower ends up a suffering fool due to his belief in separateness and "owned knowing." ALL you say ""I know" about other than I AM is complete ignorance. The only thing worth knowing is, I DON'T KNOW. There is a huge gift in Unknowing, inconceivable to the mind.

Q: What I can't say is that I'm not suffering. For a couple of years now, I have had an almost permanent tension headache.

C. You may also need medical help for that. Pain medication, chiropractic, I do not know … but I suggest you get some medical advice about that one too. Pain is a happening that goes with the living organism and can be dealt with by doctors. What I point to as suffering is different from pain; suffering is the ego's conviction that PAIN SHOULD NOT BE. It is a concept-overlay, a story that judges happenings as good or bad, right or wrong, should or should not. Pain is not really a spiritual problem. Suffering is another matter and is dealt with through investigation, but starting from the BRUTE FACT that Bare Space-Like Naked Being-Existence IS and you are THAT. Stay with this. Stay with the Know-ING, I AM. Existence IS and I Am That. Nothing but That.

Q: It often feels like something is about to give way (another writer described being 'sucked into a void') but it never does.

C. That's what happened for that appearance and who knows what will happen next in "you" or any other appearance! Nobody knows. And the description is NOT a prescription! If you think that has to happen you'll wait forever. There is NO way to control or predict ANYTHING. That's the big secret that nobody tells ya: Nobody knows anything. All that is appearing has already happened by the "time" it's perceived. We show up as observer-players of an ever-changing movie and fail to notice that we are merely characters in the movie and no more able to control the movie than and ant or a tree could control the appearing show. The perspectiveless seeing here is that all we see and know is memory and imagination.

Reminder:

Warning

Nothing in this book is real.

Nothing in this book is true.

This book points to something you do not know that you do not know. That is not a thing that words can describe, evoke, or represent.

Without one or more of those, what is left?

Nothing.

Also "known" by "no-one" as

Paradise.

The Home You Never Left.

Q: How do I tell the truth from the false?

C. That's easy. It's ALL false. Like my buddy Werner sometimes said, *"All there IS is Bullshit, and Nothin'..."!*

And my dear friend John Greven, author of "Oneness," notes: "Here's a *'Litmus Test' - If ANYTHING is assumed to be other than bullshit – then there is something wrong with the perspective".*

Full Stop.

This Is LOVE

Don't believe ANY of this: LOOK. See if you can find ANYTHING that is not either memory arising and appearing presently or imagination arising and appearing presently.

Q: There seems there are a number of people who have contacted you who have talked about suicide. I often long for death and as you say, I really hope that I do die soon.

C. Again: You cannot kill your Self. No shit. You cannot kill space. How could you annihilate No Thing? Dying happens every second, every instant ... every split second time appears and disappears as the still-yet-changing frame-by-frame. Self-Awareness is that screen on which these images appear and disappear ... the appearing happening so fast we don't notice that there is space between each frame. Sometimes the film speed slows down and you get a glimpse of Nothing, that Space between thought-image-memory-appearance-frames. But even THAT is just another "happening" arising in Aware Presence. Your True Self.

So if "you" re "waiting to die," you will stay around forever or at least until the body dies, and then, who knows? Nobody knows. And many do pretend to know. I am not one of them.

Q: I don't know if anyone else would agree, but the message 'there is no-one' often leads to a feeling of depersonalisation and depression. Obviously this truth has to be seen by no-one to be liberating, otherwise there's just a permanent 'I'm screwed' feeling.

C. That is NOT NOT NOT a "TRUTH!" It is a pointer and when the ego-mind takes that to BE a "truth" that resignation and despair is damn near inevitable. While it is ultimately so that there is no person, when "the person" BELIEVES that then suicidal depression can damn well happen!

This is a perversion of the pointing, because when the expression is ONLY "that there is no-one" what is denied in that is the obvious presence of a sense-feeling-knowing that I AM, I am here, so there seems to be a me that suffers, that when told the me does not exist as an "asserted truth" rather than only as a pointer and NOT to be believed, it is just really bullshit because it fails to embrace the ABSOLUTE PARADOX that so long as it SEEMS that there is a person, rather than resign oneself to an "I am fucked" identity or even to "I am a no-one" which is just another damned identity wanting to die because it KNOWS deep down that it is being inauthentic (!) then the paradoxically disillusioning of the non-existent ego becomes impossible owing to the fact that the investigation, the looking for the separate self-center, is refused because of this BELIEF in "there being no-one."

It really SEEMS that there IS someone there as long as it seems there is someone there! Investigation MUST happen in those cases where there is still identification as a separate entity. The root cause of suffering ultimately consists in ignoring the pointer to LOOK and ASK, ask what IS this I? Where IS this "me?" Etc. I'd suggest get real about all this. Suffering continues as a call to investigate, NOT resign oneself to a life of quiet (or loud) desperation! As far as the "feeling of depersonalization, it's only when you make the emptiness of Aware Being mean something about "you" that its depressing. Depressing to WHOM? That's the question you need to ask yourself.

Q: I'd appreciate any thoughts you have. Hope you're well, and keep the YouTube videos coming, I always enjoy them.

C. All is effortlessly resolved in The Unborn. Don't sell out on Aliveness. Selling The Unborn for thoughts and stories of a phantom "I" is like selling a diamond for the price of spinach! Just keep going and stay in touch. Much Love and Respect to you, my friend.

85. It's An Open Secret

I.M. Writes, Long time no write! I finally got around to listening the Hardball recording and some of the messages you received and I just had to write to you. ABSOLUTELY BLOODY SPOT ON!!!!

I feel so sorry for all of those people locked into the "spiritual practice" dream who seriously believe that it is making them peaceful or on their way to "enlightenment" or whatever crap they have been led to believe. And then when they still feel like shit, decide that suicide is the only option left!!! How sad!! The absolute peace and clarity they seek is already present, the open secret, but they either can't see it or just can't accept that it is their belief that they really do exist as somebody that is standing right in the way of seeing the absolute absence of their REAL presence!! Your message that you can't kill "you" by committing suicide is just brilliant. Pure wisdom!! If it is really understood. I think that the problem may be in the use or meaning of some of the words you used - "life", "death", "you" etc. because you aren't using those words to mean what most people think they mean!!! The "you" that thinks and wants to commit suicide is not the "you" that you are talking about and the "you" that you are referring to is not what they take themselves to be!!!

It is hardly surprising however that this is difficult to hear because it is the complete negation of everything we have come to believe in and hold onto. But rather than let the blast wave blow all that away and leave them seeing the total simplicity of complete absent presence, they get angry and criticise you for playing hardball!! Amazing!!

C. Yes, it IS amazing. All the Wonder of This Dream! Like a roller-coaster... It is great to hear from you again ... glad you appreciate the space that "hardball" came out of. You are expressing beautifully here, clear and authentic, from that exact same Nondual Space, as always. I appreciate the "friendship!"

86. Look For That Which Says 'I Exist'

Q: I exist. So what is there to look for?

C. The I that says "I exist." Never finding any separate I, you see directly that the one-letter word "I" is a label, a word pointing. Pointing to what? NO THING. This No Thing is the Existing-Knowing. Pure and simple, blank and empty. In that, abiding as that, there is no possibility for any suffering.

Q: That said, I must add that there's no awareness of being everything or nothing or love or life or anything like that.

And that story arises IN the Blank Luminous Awareness you ARE, the Space-like Essence of all, which silently witnesses all that arises and subsides, deep sleep, dream, waking dream ... all happens or appears IN Space-Like Awareness. This Awareness is the Silent Seer. Beyond knower and known is This Knowing Alive Presence. You Are THAT...

Stay with what IS the only unchanging actuality in your own direct experiencing: I AM – The Space of Awareness Only That - and NOT the THOUGHT I Am. If there is an expectation of some experience-state of love or nothing or everything, then that story IS also what is arising in awareness ... and, that expectation will NOT be met. Why? Any expectation depends on "becoming" and "someday." Both those concepts are stories or assumed beliefs, along with the assumption of a false "me" that hopes and wishes for some better "future." The Matrix.

This keeps the seeker in chains presently, so to speak ... yet, that too is an appearing-to-happen in empty meaningless space-like Being (code names, I AM or True-Nature.)

Q: There is just a seeing that a search is pointless and a there's a lot more acceptance of what is. It's very hard to talk about because it's like I'm channel surfing. Channel 1: M.L. seeking (and writing emails). Channel 2: There's nothing to say because it's ok. Sometimes it's like having both channels on at the same time, superimposed.

So this is the appearance, and that all arises in this Presence, The I AM-Being, The Naked Presence. Words point to NOTHING. You are that Nothing.

Q: This started yesterday after a big energy shift happened. My mind was like, "something's different, something's different," but couldn't see what.

C. That's the happening of the energetic contraction into a seeming "entity" which is a ghost-like appearance imagined to be solid and real dissolving naturally and effortlessly as Oneness Herself burns away the false ... that is of course merely a story about a happening and ultimately irrelevant. And that too shows up as an appearance to what you actually are ... Unchanging Being.

87. When "The Seeking Hasn't Stopped"

Q: The seeking hasn't stopped. I know that I exist, but I don't know what I am (or am not, as the case may be). Channel 1 is frustrated by this. Channel 2 doesn't care. I always like talking to you, even when I'm worried you're going to play hardball with me (sometimes you do, sometimes you don't).

C. Not to "hardball you" but, so what? What's appearing is what's appearing. What's so. Also so what!?

Stay with what you know. What is undeniable? You are. That I AM is Consciousness, Awareness IS and "I AM" is the pointer concept pointing at that. This Consciousness is Awareness itself, it is universal, everyone IS this and the test for this is in seeing you cannot get away from being-consciousness-awareness. Awareness is NOT an "object that can be experienced!" It's not YOUR awareness. It's Empty Universal Meaninglessness. That point is being overlooked in what you share as what's so for you... seeing this, it is seen that Consciousness is not personal. All experiencers are different, all experiences are different. All these bodyminds labeled with names, you or me, these forms, are always changing. All the experiences are ever-changing. Change is the only constant in the dream.

Seeking is the best most perfect way to keep yourself
from finding the Home you never left.

- From I Am to I Am

88. Seeking Ends In This

M.F. writes a Follow-up: Thanks for the many replies to my ego-based ramblings. After reading them all, and sitting with the pointers, and trying to "just be" this was seen: Presence-Awareness is what is illuminating everything. The deepest, most "egoic" moments of suffering are only known through this Awareness. Everything exists within it. Although "I" believed that distracting thoughts blocked "my" awareness, they were actually illuminated by it, and could not have existed outside of it. The "me who I thought I was" also exists in the same Awareness. It has all along. Everything is simply allowed; even false identification and stupidity. There is no being aware...You simply are aware!

C. YES. Awesome! Just one little "tweak" bubbles up here ... It is not actually that "you" are aware ... it is that there is Awareness, and "you" are an appearance IN that. It's not "my" awareness or "your" awareness.... it is unbounded impersonal emptiness filled with loving to be...

Anyway that is obviously preaching at the choir! As you noted, Although "I" believed that distracting thoughts blocked "my" awareness, they were actually illuminated by it, and could not have existed outside of it.

This all sounds really great! Well done!

Look now: What NEVER changes?

Formless Being. Empty Meaningless Witnessing Consciousness (a label for the Pure Being) … "I AM" … This is NO Thing and the mind-feeling story can never grasp that. Trying to grasp this IS frustration. There is no control anywhere over any of this appearance, it happens and the idea of a person as an experiencer called "me" shows up after the fact as an overlay. This is how investigating works: When you look for a controlling personal willing entity you come up empty. This, Being Empty, IS your True Nature.

Stop here at I AM. Stay with that and refuse to entertain the story that follows the simple pointer, I AM. That's all there is to this seeing-knowing. The search ends as it started … all by itself. Meanwhile stay with this pure I AM, witnessing all that is. Be what you are, and refuse all identification as anything else but that.

- From I Am to I Am

89. One To One

J.H. shares, Good Morning Charlie, The other evening while viewing one of your You-tube conversations filling up my monitor with your talking head as I gazed into your eyes, I experienced Truth. Consciousness was communicating directly to Consciousness for there was no Charlie and there was no Jeff listening and viewing Charlie. The experience in the limited communication of words was pure Oneness, just pure Oneness. Smiles!!

C. Welcome to the Home You never left! Now, stay Present to the fact that the "experience of Oneness' arises and subsides in what You are ... Bare Naked Awareness. THAT never changes. THAT thou art. Nothing else. Nothing that comes and goes passes the test of Ultimate Reality. Not to preach to the choir; just a "cautionary" pointer. Love ya!

Nothing ever really happened at all. There were only appearances arising and setting in the perfect clarity that you have never been separate from, because it is what you are.

- John Wheeler

You Are What You Seek

- From I Am to I Am

This is it. I Am. There's no separate self to realize. There's nothing to do, nowhere to go—this is it!

-Stephen Wingate

90. There Is No God AND You Are God

Q: We don't know all is God because all is God. LOL. If all is movement, how would we even know all is movement without some still "point" at which to judge from? If all is noise, how would we even know noise without a "point" at which to judge from? If we were all thoughts, we wouldn't even know thoughts unless there was "a part of us" that was not. We are bassackwards :) Only god can see god. If all was blue, some wise guy might come along and speak about this "something" that is called blue, and everyone would be looking for it or something. But all they see is blue, then they ask the question, what is blue. to no avail... anywho, just a child's thoughts... a reply would be greatly appreciated.

C. There is NO GOD … and … YOU ARE GOD.

This is Nothing arising as Everything, appearing separate and seeming personal until it isn't. God, how wild is that!? Thanks you for Your Silence, I AM.

There is absolutely NOTHING TO GET.

(And no one to get this no thing!)

Got it?

Drop It!

Thanks for sharing! Thanks for BEING. Thanks for nothing … that's the supreme unknowable aliveness that you are in reality.

Acceptance is not something you do.

It's what you are.

- John Astin

I Yam what I Yam

- Popeye

91. What Is Seeking Who?

Many say "I have been seeking". That is not true! There is no I apart from all that is; that "I" you claim as an identity is nothing but a thought that comes and goes in awareness. And the concept I points to No Thing - That no thing is simple Awareness, Presence, Being. That is NOT a concept. I as a concept points to that awareness. Like air as a concept points to the stuff that the body breathes in and out. Can't see air but it IS. Obviously. Can't see awareness - that IS ... obviously. IT IS and IS what you are.

Seeking is a story added to that I that is just an assumed identity and that identity is just flat false. What is TRUE? Who are you really? That assumption of being an "I" apart IS the assumed separateness and it is ALL just a bunch of thoughts. Whether any thoughts or stories are here or not awareness is simply never missing, never changes. This understanding is simplicity itself: That awareness is what you are, silent, clear, empty, all embracing stillness in which sounds and movements arise. Take your stand as I AM Awareness and refuse the mind's stance or positionality "I am I, me, separate from awareness". How can any appearance, any thought, any story actually be separate from awareness? Nothing can appear unless the No Thing of awareness is. Awareness is here now, first and foremost. Who can't see that awareness is never missing?

Don't mistake what you are – awareness – to be a thing apart from itself. You are No Thing. Only That!

Keep coming back to the simplicity of that which is aware. Right now you are aware of these words. This awareness that's looking out through your eyes is Love. Thoughts, feelings, stories, and dramas all appear to you. You are the Love you're seeking. We are all seeking Love. The great and liberating realization is that we are the Love we are seeking, and it is always here. Just notice—I am the Love I'm seeking. I am Love. I Am.

-Stephen Wingate

92. Ego Plays A Waiting Game FOREVER

Q: There is still no sense or "shift" to the being or noticing of the "space" as the reality. I know you either is or you ain't in regards to dropping of this sense of separation and clear seeing. My deep feeling is "who cares" as it's only the ego that wants this (funny, the ego wanting its own demise). Is this simple awareness there is the sensing of something aware of "me" being aware, the knowing that there is acceptance happening without an acceptor. When looking inward for a "me", empty space is all that is perceived, yet no cigar! What is missing? Awareness still seems to be felt within the space in my skull, although it is known to encompass it and everything else, including these thoughts. It still feels like winning the "booby prize" but with bits of clear seeing or knowing here and there.

C. You are the man who knew too much, my friend. You say, "There is still no sense or "shift" to the being or noticing of the "space." YOU CANNOT GET AWAY FROM Being-Space. And if you are waiting for a "shift" you are gonna wait FOREVER. That is not a person's Reality … not anyone's Reality. That IS Unaware-Of-Itself Reality... for no one and everyone. All else is a bullshit story the mind tells itself. It is all self-reinforcing ... tautological! The perceiver you still take yourself to be that "perceives" empty space is the false sense of being separate and that asserts itself due to lack of deep investigation. WHO or WHAT IS that "perceiver?"

LOOK ... RIGHT NOW … Who is writing all that? Who types, who thinks, who are you to yourself and for yourself? What do you take your self to be? Everything appears and unappears IN Awareness. That is NEVER absent. These " bits of clear seeing or knowing here and there" arise and subside IN what You are. This what you are is NOT an object you can grasp or know. You are chasing your own tail. LOOK: There is noticing or seeing or knowing that or not, arising IN that. This Being IS and cannot be denied or attained by thought. IT IS. So what? Who cares?

All that is happening is you take a thought, a story and a storyteller, which is a temporary appearance in what You are, to

209

be the actual ... there is no person, only a thought of a "me." LOOK for this me rather than buying the false assertion of thought reinforcing itself in an endless suffering tautology.

There is nowhere to go and nothing to get!

That's all there is to get.

Little "me" or little "you" are waves denying their essence as ocean. It's ignorance coupled with arrogance... divine perfect being arising as ignorance and arrogance. It's LOVELY!

DROP IT ALL AND DWELL IN AND AS NOT KNOWING, CLUELESS TIMELESS BEING. Perfect Peace. This is the Real You... The Unborn Presence of Being. Here and now you are THAT and THAT Alone (All One.) Do not trade the Unborn Aliveness of NON-conceptual Awakeness for the paltry little thoughts of a "me" that is but a phantom. You take a ghost to be real. Correcting that error is what Nonduality points to.

When looking inward for a "me", empty space is all that is perceived, yet no cigar! what is missing?

That empty Space IS your True Self. THAT is never missing. It is not that there is anything missing ... it's that there is a still a false sense of "me" wanting more or better or different than the Emptiness of Being-Awareness-Peace.

There are no spiritual cookies on offer here. No kidding ... there is NOTHING to get.

Got that? :-)

Finally, LOOK ... Realize ... NOW ... if you had a choice, you would NEVER give up the ghost; NEVER let go of the illusion of "being a person." So: While there IS no choice, if you believe you are real and can choose, as it seems to you that "you" are a chooser-doer, then do this, INVESTIGATE. Who IS this "me?" WHAT IS IT? WHERE IS IT?

Find out right now.

Part Three: Paradise Found

Just notice, I am aware. Notice the awareness that you are—not the concept of awareness. If you can hear anything, see anything, feel anything—it's the awareness that's hearing, seeing, and feeling. Awareness is timelessly present. It's not yesterday, it's not tomorrow. It's always now. You don't have to wait five minutes, nor can you go back in time five minutes. It's this point of timeless, spaceless awareness that's always seeing, hearing, tasting, touching, smelling.

–Stephen Wingate

93. All Done, All One, Forever Home

A Last Follow-up from A.S.R.: Hello Charlie, I've arrived at home, the home I never left. It's all been seen, is being seen. It's seen that it's always been this way. Thank you, you dear piece of oneness for your audio asking your callers "What wakes you up in the morning?". As soon as I heard that question, "I don't know" filled the mind and left these lips. And in a crazy moment there was a knowing that I didn't KNOW anything. What wakes me in the morning, where my feelings come from, where my thoughts come from.... There wasn't a clue.

The mind gave up.

And "I" (LOL, gotta use the word for convenience) clearly saw and (the seeing goes on) that pain, jealousy, anger, embarrassment, joy, bliss, elation: these all arise for no reason whatsoever and they always did, for absolutely NO ONE. And the doubt, which kept coming back and back (and still does) is arising for NO ONE. The frustration at "not getting something" had nothing to do with a "me". It was simply a feeling arising in tandem with an arising thought. And frustration still arises, but it is clearly seen: It arises for absolutely NO ONE. And "my" life goes on exactly as before. A freakin' paradox! Love, A

C. Yes! Welcome To Paradise - The Home You Never Left.

Much Love to you, dear ONE.

""'Advaita' is not two. When you see that you know nothing and there is not two—that's it. There's nothing left to do.

-Stephen Wingate

Without conceptual thoughts, there is no suffering. Can you see this, really see this?

– John Wheeler

94. Paradox & Confusion

The mind sees contradiction where what is actually arising is PARADOX. The essence of the paradox of nonduality is that a) there is no person and b) so long as there is the assumption, the belief, that you are a person inquiry is advised.

While in truth there is no person, until that is the Being-Actuality and NOT merely a belief in being no-one, some intervention is advised by those who have seen the Real and discarded the false and are encouraging you to do the same, in various ways unique to the particular organism's expression of the inexpressible.

In my view all those you name are in this category.

SIT with the paradox. Be with this paradox. Don't try to resolve it; let it sit there like a brick in your lap. See what crumbles as this is sat with so to speak.

It is an old pointer that "the guardians at the gateless gate of Truth are Paradox and Confusion". Confusion is NOT KNOWING. Be in Not Knowing. Be with the Paradox.

When this stuff was pointed out to me, it became clear that the person "John Wheeler" simply did not exist, except as an assumption. There may be discernable personality traits of the body-mind, but they are entirely irrelevant to what I am.

-John Wheeler

Yes. That also says it for "charlie".

95. Thanks for The No-Bullshit Approach

Q: As usual you cut through the bullshit and pull no punches. There is so much shit out there. I spent some time with the teachings from a guy in California who talks about past lives and how we can "heal" ourselves. I tuned into a live conference of his on the internet a while ago and left after half an hour after hearing enough bullshit. These guys keep stringing people along promising enlightenment and paradise. Just keep paying and someday you'll get it!

C. Yep, that's the Great Con game of "conceptual enlightenment" ... the myth of "someday."

Q: Anyway, keep up the good work,

C. Nobody doing it! Anyway, Welcome To Paradise!

96. Consciousness In Drag

Q: Hi, Charlie...and even the ego illusion is Consciousness in disguise...;-)

C. Absolutely!! (Relatively speaking!!) Love ya ...

Here is a great pointer from *Robin Dale*

(http://nonduality.com/robindale.htm)

"There is only This. If you think you're enlightened, throw it away and begin again. The idea of 'enlightenment' is like a big ugly monster with a pretty face, inside you. Like the idea of the Abyss is a big warm openhearted angel with an ugly face".

Exactly. The only way we lost paradise is by seeking it! I am in Paradise and I am not in Paradise are BOTH false!

This as it is, IS Paradise.

Here. Now. .... The Lost and Found Department in This Paradise is CLOSED, once and FOR GOOD.

97. The Real Deal

B.C. Offers the perspective of one "in the trenches:" It is nice to hear someone apply some non-duality to suicide. Ain't no one here to kill. Never was. It is nice to remember after a long week of work and stress that all of this is just a three dimensional movie that doesn't mean anything. It comes, it goes. It isn't important. Nothing is important, so just enjoy the ride. A seeker wrote you and clamed he was going to kill himself in some specified future time! So he claimed.

Most of the people "I" deal with as a 911 operator want to kill themselves right now. Then police, fire department and ambulance rush out there to help keep that person alive so he can suffer a little while longer....hahaha... People who aren't ready to "die" call someone to say they want to kill their self. People who WERE ready to die are found dead by their relatives. But "you" know that. And none of this is important. This whole existence is just an illusion and there is no me sending an email to a you and this whole exercise is a waste of fucking time because "I" could have been playing 'World of Warcraft' for the last hour...hahaha. Have a good day!

C. Bang on! Thanks for this sharing The Love.

Everywhere and Everything

As you are looking out through your eyes at these words, you are looking out into your own mind. Your mind is three-dimensional space. Your mind is this computer screen. Your mind is the space between your eyes and this computer screen. Everywhere you look you are looking into your own mind. Your mind is not in your head; your head is in your mind. Everything you see, hear, feel, conceive and experience is your own mind.

Look around the room where you are right now—you are looking into your own mind. Your own mind IS the world. Your mind is three-dimensional space and time. Everywhere you look, you are looking into your own mind. As you look at your hand, your hand is your own mind. The space between your fingers is your own mind. The wall is your own mind. The space between your eyes and the wall is your own mind. Your own mind is every object you see, and your own mind is the space between every object you see.

"Everywhere you look, you are looking into your own mind. Your own mind is everywhere and everything. Everywhere and everything is your own mind.

-Stephen Wingate

Part Four: The End Of Becoming

The TRUE "end game" consists NOT in rooting out the ego or dismissing the "I" thought as "not me." The final stroke comes in simply seeing what you already always ARE. Being IS and there is no escape from That, nor any possibility of attaining That. You ARE.

Can you deny that this Isness IS obviously Present and Aware, open, empty and clear? It is the most available and undeniable space. IT IS. That was never lost. You are That. That's all there is to this - Seeing what was never absent and always completely free.

- From I Am to I Am

98. This Is Paradise

Q: A few days after our talk, after I stated I felt like "plain oatmeal and was just exhausted." You suggested just sit with that. All I did was sit with it. In fact that's all I COULD do. No choice involved. I was just there sitting with all the exhaustion. Then I sat with other things that begin to arise. Emotions, thoughts. I would get up and just be with it. Again, that's all I COULD do. Then one night while driving, I was just sitting with thoughts that were arising. And there was the sense that I was sitting with not only sitting with thoughts and observing them but there was the sense of sitting with the "I" sense and presence. Just as if there is this "person" and it was the real "me" that was sitting with everything was open, wide peaceful nothingness observing the little invented "I' Very hard to describe this. Anyway, the openness and peaceful nothing that was observing this "I" energy is what has remained. And whenever the thoughts come up or a worry about "me" comes up it seems to have as much validity as thinking something like...."I wonder if Santa Claus is cold." I don't feel like "I've got it". If I were pressed to say anything ... about "spiritual path progress" I would have to say, "I've lost it."

C. BINGO!

Q: There is just nothing that seems as serious or important as it used to. There are times of course the thoughts cause an emotion but it quickly passes through as it is sat with. OK. I guess, you're thinking "Gee I just asked "How you were?" "It wasn't an essay question girl." LOL - But I wanted to share. :) Thanks for listening.

C. This is all very, very beautiful. The conclusion, "I lost it all." As has been pointed out, until the idea that it's "my" life has been lost there is always doubt, confusion, seeking and suffering. You are Life Itself. Now, that's known by no-one and that is absolute freedom. Well done. Welcome To Paradise Found! Love ya!

99. It Takes No Effort To Be The Self

Q: Ahhhhh, sweet home. The effort is to stay "out" of the Real. To be OneSelf .... nothing is required. I don't find the words to express that .... awaking from a dream is the LIVE. And if the dream is a nightmare............. awaking [to that dream] is [seemingly] needed. Thank you for your help, because I think the help is really more inside than a book. And you send me the book but send me too a lot of more. If there is no one, the imagined boundaries are no problem.

C. Very well stated. Welcome to the Home you never left ... your Real Self, infinite, unbounded and supremely FREE. I Love You.

100. Realization Happens Naturally

Q: It dawned on me this morning that maybe it is the I that believes it is seeing I am nothing, rather than nothing seeing it is nothing.

C. That is what's happening. This is "knowing I am nothing" and is a step into Being and back into "me." There is nothing that needs to be "done about that." Realization of Being Nothing comes about naturally just like breathing. This "stage" is one where it's still "means something" that life and you are empty and meaningless. No worries, all is ultimately resolved (dissolved) in The Unborn. Nothing cannot see itself as nothing! Space cannot divide itself to "know itself." All the tail chasing the seeker is caught up in happens all by itself and the end happens all by itself. Hearing and seeing this there may be a relaxing about it all. In the final seeing no-one sees. In the ultimate knowing no-one knows. THIS is the open secret that nobody knows. You are I. I is you. You are all. All is not therefore it is. Words!

It is empty and meaningless that it's empty and meaningless.

Q: ... and then there was word :-) ....yours have such authenticity, thank you for sharing......

C. Really it is Nothing :-).

There will never BE "realization" for "you!" Look again: WHO gets involved? Involvement happens. That's LIFE! The false overlay of an "owner-manager-doer" called "I" that assumes IT is "involved" is simply not being seen for what it is ... a story arising and subsiding again in Awareness. Your real natural state of Being IS that Awareness and NOT the "content" – the I thought – that is mistakenly taken to be who you are. It's simple: YOU IS. Everything ... all the stories, emotions, thoughts, identifications as a thought, a name, a form arises and disappears IN that Is-ness, like storms in an ever-empty untouchable space of clear shining sky.

- From I Am to I Am

101. Call It Grace

Q: Wow, it's like all is a movement of call it "Grace". I'm fascinated. All happens at the right moment, not before, not after. Your presence is tangible. Yes. Many thanks. It's wonderful to remove the cataracts of ignorance. You can spend all your existence rejoicing in the embrace of God. Why I should doubt, than I'm other than God? Why doubt that He is the Only and the One ever? In all forms, without a form, embracing, swinging, breastfeeding, birthing, dying, and yet, remaining THE SAME. Much Love, Yours in One...

C. This is IT!

Only Love is Real and You are That ...

... now it's known.

In Timeless Respect and Love,

102. "Oneness Re-Cognizing Its Self"

Q: I think you have hit on some important points that I was missing. Every time I re-read your pointers, more is understood and some resonance is struck. When searching before with naked awareness, no "me" was seen. I guess that the ego was only playing hide and seek and was thought to be banished!

Accepting things as they appear in the moment, without judgment by the mind is also understood, but as you said, there is apparently quite a bit of "me" left to resist it, and cause suffering. In truth, there may be only intellectual agreement that "Awareness" is my true nature, although it is seen so bright and clear. You are right.

C. "Along the way" that all happened here as well. It was very much the same … it's apparently pretty common. It was immediately clear when John Wheeler pointed it out in my first phone consultation with him (prompted by the crystal clarity of his writings.) But then the reassertion of the me, unnoticed but still in play, showed up as suffering. It was frustrating as hell because the clear seeing HAD happened and so the suffering coming back was a bit of a bear. Subsequent conversations with John and Bob Adamson cleared it up.

The apparent ego was so stubborn that (unlike you) I stopped listening for a while. But after going to Melbourne to visit with Bob Adamson, gradually the subtle remnants of the false self-center were seen trough and there was less and less fixation.

The pointer regarding this from Nisargadatta is, "suffering is a call for investigation." To me the fact of suffering still happening is the proof that the fixation on an entity called "myself" is still in play, as you are now seeing. So the antidote is investigation! Exploring this with someone who no longer has that false belief can often be the final step. That was the case for me as I discussed these things with the true Friend, the One appearing as (primarily) John Wheeler, Bob Adamson, and John Greven.

However let's be clear: This is ultimately a function of Oneness Recognizing ItSelf!

In the words of John Wheeler, "The first expression of the unconditioned is the sense of being that is conscious of itself. This self-shining consciousness, or pure sense of "I am", knows all else and also knows itself. It is the self-knowing light in which manifestation appears. The light of consciousness emerges from a source that cannot be described or named. Nothing at all can be predicated of that primordial reality. It cannot even be said to be or be conscious. It is the ultimate subjectivity, which cognizes even the sense of being, consciousness and peace."

Being, Consciousness, Peace or Existingness-Awareness-Aliveness... As in the Sanskrit, Sat-Chit-Ananda. Not three not two not one. THIS is what You are. Start with That ... and Stop with That.

103. Everything Is Being

Being Is all there ever was is will be and not a thing or even no thing exists that is NOT Being. Being divine, being mundane. Being bondage, Being Liberation, Being Ignorance and Being Wisdom. All there is, is Being. Who says they are not Being? What claims to be separate from being? Only Being.

No Way Out, No Way In, No Way Through.

Paradise.

This too is Being, Being One, Being Many, Being the nothing of empty meaningless Space, Being Time, Being yesterday tomorrow today.

There is ONLY Being. You are both That and Not That. This is IT and that's That. Love hate War Peace Nothing Everything.

No being does being. Only Being Is.

104. This Is A Natural Functioning

Q: Logically, I cannot be anything I can think. If I can think it, I cannot be it. Even the mind can see this. So thinking about this blows my mind for awhile, then I have to get back to work and in a jiffy am back to (the habit of) believing I'm these thoughts! Amazing.

C. Believing "I am these thoughts?" Is that true? The real test as far as I can tell is, are you suffering with these beliefs in thoughts? Or is there just a naturally functioning brain that is able to do its work without a concern like "am I doing it right?" In the absence of these me-myself worry-overlays the brain thinks and acts naturally, perfectly well, as Consciousness operates through it and all is well as work is done by no doer. Get what I am pointing to? No problem with thoughts and beliefs so long as there's no suffering! The "me" of a natural functioning organism is not a problem, not at all.

But then who or what IS this "I" you say you are several times? And "my?" Who owns the thoughts? Who owns the work? IS there an owner?? Seeing through the I and seeing that what you are is the Aware-Presence that the one-letter label "I" points to is what we share here.

105. Original Sin? Ignoring The One True Self

D.S. Writes, I awakened to the Nondual a little over 2 years ago while in India. Life is much simpler when there is know one that takes it seriously anymore. I joke with people saying that the meditative God seeker named D. went to India but never came back; he is probably still there seeking. I wanted to share with you a thought that came to me a couple of weeks ago...it has to do with original sin; most Christians have the concept that everyone is sinner when born. I feel what Jesus met by that was some thing totally different. To me the one sin, if you even want to call it that but I will in this context, is overlooking the Self that we truly are. Karma can only affect you when you identified with body or even the soul. Suffering only hurts when there is a someone to suffer...

C. "My view" on this is that "original sin" (which many translate as "mistake" or "to miss the mark") is simply, as you say, erroneously overlooking the natural ever-present Being-Awareness which alone is what is Real. I would add that taking the thought "I am" to be "me" - seemingly displacing the Nondual Space-Like I AM of Non-conceptual Being - to be the key mistake in this illusory world-appearance... believing "I am" a thought, a name, a form, a body, IS the mistake and when that is what we take the self to be, suffering is inevitable. Seeing that the belief is false ends the confusion and leaves what already always IS ... Being-Awareness-Peace.

Anyway, all sounds right on. No D.S., no suffering! This is Being, Home in the Heart Land. Thanks for sharing that!

106. Pain – an Invitation To Paradise

Q: I am in great pain that medications no longer ease. What do I really need to understand to see that I am not responsible for this pain - that I am not the feeler or the experiencer of this pain?

C. The understanding is less valuable than your actual experience. Did you create the pain? Did you create the body that is enduring pain? Did you create your parents? Look in actual experience, NOT some "spiritual story" or seminar leader assertion that "you are responsible, you cause your own pain. THAT is some truly evil bullshit.

As to correctly understanding this happening: All stories are imagination. Experience alone is real in your own case. Do not buy any imaginary story of being responsible! If YOU are responsible for making the pain happen, and you do not want this pain. HOW could you ever believe you are the cause of something you clearly do NOT want? It's absolutely illogical to assume that the thought of a "me" can do or cause a damn thing!

What are you in Truth? Who is the "person" who you assume you are that owns pain? Keep investigating that as best you can. This pain may just be your "personal invitation" to Paradise.

107. Body Identification Is Suffering

To paraphrase Nisargadatta Maharaj, Krishnamurti talks about the total manifestation, while I point out that which brought the manifest into existence. Whatever is being done, if you think you are the doer, it's the ego.

Krishnamurti is not a person; he is in that state which is described (only described!) as the stateless state of Eternal Isness.

The Supreme being is Everywhere and Nowhere … appearing as everything and every "one".

Intellectual experiences apart, most people only want some benefit through the body. Instead of only deriving benefit through the body, stabilize in yourself, if your true identify is not realized, you will die with the body identity and name.

The knowledge 'I am' is at the very centre. From where do you experience the manifest world and body? Is it not because of the centre? If the centre 'I am' did not exist, would you experience the body? Give up the identity that you are a woman [or a man]; attachment to male or female forms is itself an illusion.

108. Soul or Sole ... All One

Q: I was reading your site and I like it a lot. This Advaita approach is beautiful, simple and direct. and it cuts through a lot of crap! :) However, sometimes I get the feeling that Advaita goes a bit too far and throws the baby out with the bath water. The baby, what is the baby? Maybe you could call it the "inner me" or the "soul". What I mean is, I feel an inner richness now that I, as far as I remember, didn't feel when I was much younger, in my early twenties, let's say. Concrete memories fade but something remains; their essence. And this essence is 'me', the 'soul' that I am. I am indeed not the 'person', the main character in the movie of this life. But on the other hand, I'm also not only an empty mirror, pure awareness, tabula rasa or whatever. Sure, I am that, but I am also more, 'me' is more. I'm not only spirit, so to speak, I'm also soul, this soul. And this soul, unlike the person, is real, it has substance. Or so it seems! :). My question is, I guess, is there any place for this 'inner me' in your approach?

C. Thanks for Being-In-Touch. :-) As Nisargadatta said, and is the experience of this here, when I know I am nothing that is wisdom; when I know I am everything that is Love. And this Life moves between these two. Life, not "my life.")

To me, the "I Am Everything" is what you're trying to say is the "soul." That is IM-personal, Universal, Eternally bright and clear. I like to change the spelling to point to how it's seen "here:" SOLE.

One. Sole. That is what is pointed to with these words. Nothing, Being Everything.

So we basically agree. The recognition of True-Nature Isness ... call it Soul or Sole ... is Being-Awareness-Aliveness, easy and peaceful in itself as itself. One-Without-A-Second.

Q: Thank you for answering! :) Yes, what Nisargadatta said, I encountered that same quote a few weeks ago and, well, yes, yes ... See, I'm running out of words again, and not only because English is not my first language. Can't say it, can you? Yes, we agree. :) Thank you, love you!

109. In The End: It's Heart To Heart

Q: As is known, it is tough to express oneself when dealing with the subject of Advaita because nothing is happening, and there is no you. That being said, I would like you to know how much the conference call was appreciated. That was the first time that I had direct verbal contact with a teacher. That is important because, as I have read (over and over) and as stated by yourself: Direct contact seems to be of more value than books. I got off the phone feeling, for lack of a better term, lighter, and with the feeling of things resonating.

C. Sounds good, my friend. Stay with the simplicity of this Aliveness, let it erase the false, leaving what already IS ... YOU: Being-Awareness, filling the space that is with Aliveness.

Part Five - Last Words

Words! Words!
The Way is beyond language,
for in it there is no yesterday,
　　no tomorrow
　　　　no today.

- Seng T'san

Grace Is This

G. shares, Thought just occurring...

... to have the seeker claim, it 'gets it', is the dreamer, dreaming it's awake. Yet Presence through conscious awareness sees the happenings arising and falling... revealing the fact that a dream person never existed.

C. Nice!

Search Cancelled – Seeker Gone

Q: I was going to go to Sedona Arizona to see [a teacher] this week, but canceled. There just wasn't the drive, the necessity. Although I would have enjoyed it, the search ended after my phone call to you. It's true that the search can end. Not that I don't still enjoy reading a good non dual book or blog. And I still very much enjoy [that author], but there is just no drive for searching. The answer IS. It was so wonderful that you were there to take my call and end this seeker.

C. Yes, as always, the best news is NO news and the Recognition that there IS no one to be driven ever again!

Beyond concepts of either power or force, here you are!

It Is Said

There are two "Guardians"

at the Gateless Gate to Paradise:

Confusion

And

Paradox.

Love them Unconditionally

Pet them and allow them to snarl

Love Them Completely

and they will lovingly let you pass

through the

transparent doorway

to The Home You never Left

Just Now. ....

Empty Mind, Zen Mind

(Excerpted from "No Way Out" by Charlie Hayes)

"To this ultimate state, no law or description applies"

The Hsin-Hsin Ming
Verses on the Faith-Mind
By Seng Ts'an,
The Third Chinese Patriarch
Translated by Richard B. Clarke

The Great Way is not difficult
for those not attached to preferences.
When neither love nor hate arises,
all is clear and undisguised.
Separate by the smallest amount, however,
and you are as far from it as heaven is from earth.

If you wish to know the truth,
then hold to no opinions for or against anything.
To set up what you like against what you dislike
is the disease of the mind.

When the fundamental nature of things is not recognized
the mind's essential peace is disturbed to no avail.
The Way is perfect as vast space is perfect,
where nothing is lacking and nothing is in excess.

Indeed, it is due to our grasping and rejecting

that we do not know the true nature of things.

Live neither in the entanglements of outer things,

nor in ideas or feelings of emptiness.

Be serene and at one with things

and erroneous views will disappear by themselves.

When you try to stop activity to achieve quietude,

your very effort fills you with activity.

As long as you remain attached to one extreme or another

you will never know Oneness.

Those who do not live in the Single Way

cannot be free in either activity or quietude, in assertion

or denial.

Deny the reality of things

and you miss their reality;

assert the emptiness of things

and you miss their reality.

The more you talk and think about it

the further you wander from the truth.

So cease attachment to talking and thinking,

and there is nothing you will not be able to know.

To return to the root is to find the essence,

but to pursue appearances or "enlightenment" is to miss

the source.
To awaken even for a moment
is to go beyond appearance and emptiness.

Changes that seem to occur in the empty world
we make real only because of our ignorance.

Do not seek for the truth;
Only cease to cherish opinions.

Do not remain in a dualistic state;
avoid such easy habits carefully.
If you attach even to a trace
of this and that, of right and wrong,
the Mind-essence will be lost in confusion.

Although all dualities arise from the One,
do not be attached even to ideas of this One.

When the mind exists undisturbed in the Way,
there is no objection to anything in the world;
and when there is no objection to anything,
things cease to be— in the old way.
When no discriminating attachment arises,
the old mind ceases to exist.
Let go of things as separate existences
and mind too vanishes.

Likewise when the thinking subject vanishes
so too do the objects created by mind.

The arising of other gives rise to self;
giving rise to self generates others.
Know these seeming two as facets
of the One Fundamental Reality.
In this Emptiness, these two are really one—
and each contains all phenomena.
If not comparing, nor attached to "refined" and "vulgar"—
you will not fall into judgment and opinion.

The Great Way is embracing and spacious—
to live in it is neither easy nor difficult.
Those who rely on limited views are fearful and irresolute:
The faster they hurry, the slower they go.
To have a narrow mind,
and to be attached to getting enlightenment
is to lose one's center and go astray.

When one is free from attachment,
all things are as they are,
and there is neither coming nor going.

When in harmony with the nature of things, your own
fundamental nature,
and you will walk freely and undisturbed.

However, when mind is in bondage, the truth is hidden,

and everything is murky and unclear,

and the burdensome practice of judging

brings annoyance and weariness.

What benefit can be derived

from attachment to distinctions and separations?

If you wish to move in the One Way,

do not dislike the worlds of senses and ideas.

Indeed, to embrace them fully

is identical with true Enlightenment.

The wise person attaches to no goals

but the foolish person fetters himself or herself.

There is one Dharma, without differentiation.

Distinctions arise from the clinging needs of the ignorant.

To seek Mind with the discriminating mind

is the greatest of mistakes.

Rest and unrest derive from illusion;

with enlightenment, attachment to liking and disliking

ceases.

All dualities come from ignorant inference.

They are like dreams, phantoms, hallucinations—

it is foolish to try to grasp them.

Gain and loss, right and wrong;

finally abandon all such thoughts at once.

If the eye never sleeps,
all dreams will naturally cease.

If the mind makes no discriminations,
the ten thousand things
are as they are, of single essence.

To realize the mystery of this One-essence
is to be released from all entanglements.
When all things are seen without differentiation,
the One Self-essence is everywhere revealed.
No comparisons or analogies are possible
in this causeless, relationless state of just this One.

When movement stops, there is no movement—
and when no movement, there is no stopping.
When such dualities cease to exist
Oneness itself cannot exist.
To this ultimate state
no law or description applies.

For the Realized mind at one with the Way
all self-centered striving ceases.
Doubts and irresolutions vanish
and the Truth is confirmed in you.
With a single stroke you are freed from bondage;

nothing clings to you and you hold to nothing.

All is empty, clear, self-illuminating,

with no need to exert the mind.

Here, thinking, feeling, understanding, and imagination
are of no value.

In this world "as it really is"

there is neither self nor other-than-self.

To know this Reality directly

is possible only through practicing non-duality.

When you live this non-separation,

all things manifest the One, and nothing is excluded.

Whoever comes to enlightenment,

no matter when or

where,

Realizes personally this fundamental Source.

This Dharma-truth has nothing to do with big or small,
with time and space.

Here a single thought is as ten thousand years.

Not here, not there—

but everywhere always right before your eyes.

Infinitely large and infinitely small: no difference,

for definitions are irrelevant

and no boundaries can be discerned.

So likewise with "existence" and "non-existence."

Don't waste your time in arguments and discussion
attempting to grasp the ungraspable.

Each thing reveals the One,
the One manifests as all things.
To live in this Realization
is not to worry about perfection or non-perfection.
To put your trust in the Heart-Mind is to live without
separation,
and in this non-duality you are one with your Life-Source.

Words! Words!
The Way is beyond language,
for in it there is no yesterday,
no tomorrow
no today.

*Reprinted by permission of the translator, Richard B.
Clarke, director and resident teacher at the Living
Dharma Center (P.O. Box 304, Amherst, MA 01004)*

Appendix: Books, Websites and Resources

John Wheeler

Website: www.thenaturalstate.org

Books: "Awakening To The Natural State", "Right Here, Right Now", "Shining In Plain View", and "You Were never Born"

'Sailor' Bob Adamson

Website: http://members.iinet.net.au/~adamson7

Books: "What's Wrong With Right Now (Unless You Think About It"), "Presence-Awareness: Just This and Nothing Else"

Many CDs and DVDs – see the website.

Tony Parsons

Website: www.theopensecret.com

Books: "Invitation To Awaken", "As It Is", "All There Is", Nothing Being Everything"

Many CDs and DVDs – see the website.

John Greven

Website: www.onenessjustthat.com

Book: "Oneness – The Destination You never Left"

Stephen Wingate

Website: www.livinginpeace-thenaturalstate.com

Books: "The Outrageous Myths Of Enlightenment', "Dogs, Cats, & Dreams of Spiritual Awakening"

+ Many CDs and DVDs – see the website.

Annette Nibley

Website: www.whatneverchanges.com

Scott Kiloby

Website: www.kiloby.com

Book: "Love's Quiet Revolution: The End Of The Spiritual Search".

Wayne Liquorman (Ram Tzu)

Website: www.advaita.org

Books: "No Way" (Ram Tzu), "Acceptance Of What Is", and "Never Mind"

Leo Hartong

Website: www.awakeningtothedream.com

Books: "Awakening To The Dream" and "Self To Self

Randall Friend

Website: http://avastu0.blogspot.com/

Jeff Foster

Website: http://www.lifewithoutacentre.com/

Books: "Life Without A centre" and "Beyond Awakening"

Unmani (Liza) Hyde

Website: http://www.not-knowing.com/

Book: "I Am Life Itself"

John Astin

Website: www.integrativearts.com

Books: "This Is Always Enough" and "Too Intimate For Words"

Maury Lee

Website: http://nomaury.blogspot.com

Many Thanks to Pradeep Apte, aptep@yahoo.com for the quotes of Sri Nisargadatta, which he lovingly compiled and offers freely.

About The Author

Charlie Hayes, once also known as Ishan, was first a Jazz musician, then a professional racing driver, a racing cars and parts distributor, a Ferrari Dealer. Later after a devastating failure of his business he became what most call a "seeker", trying to find the source of happiness, peace and love that he felt was utterly missing despite his success and fame.

After thirty years of seeking through many paths, teachers, books and gurus, Hayes met his "final teacher", Nonduality Author John Wheeler of Santa Cruz, California in late 2004 and shortly afterwards met John's teacher, 'Sailor' Bob Adamson, in Australia.

He recalls, "John and Bob pointed out the simplicity of Being – the undeniable knowingness of the awareness called "I Am" – as the natural state of wholeness, and also pointed out that the assumed person was merely a thought that had been mistakenly identified as a self apart from Wholeness and could be seen AS false with some investigation. This put paid to the long search for Paradise in short order!"

Charlie offers meetings in Oklahoma (which are also available free of charge via conference calls), and occasionally offers talks at other locations where he is invited to share this Good News of Paradise Found. He can be reached at +1 580-366-4083, or by e-mail at non.duality@yahoo.com.

There is also a website is www.theetrnalstate.org.

All are welcome.

.

Love Is Empty, and Meaningless.

That's what makes It LOVE.

- From I Am to I Am

FULL STOP

www.ingramcontent.com/pod-product-compliance
Lightning Source LLC
LaVergne TN
LVHW011220080426
835509LV00005B/228